The Tenacity of Hope

A Devotional on Disappointments, Loss, and Everything in Between

The Tenacity of Hope

A Devotional on Disappointments, Loss, and Everything in Between

By

John C. Richards Jr.

apple**brook** Publishing

Atlanta, Georgia

Design: Kimberly Applewhite

Interior Design: Lolita Westbrook

Copyediting: Kyle Waalen

ISBN-13: 978-1615971889
ISBN-10: 0615971881

apple**brook** Publishing
Atlanta, Georgia

To my precious niece Daneé, my dear friend Monica, and my biological father, John Sr. Rest in his arms.

"I'm excited about this devotional being released to the church. With the Spirit's help, John gives us content that is theologically sound, engaging, applicable, and edifying. I am thankful God has called him to labor over the text for the benefit of the church."

Phillip Holmes
Cofounder, *Reformed African American Network (RAAN)*
Jackson, Mississippi

"John is an anointed man of God who is current and cutting edge with a kingdom message. I truly believe God has empowered John Richards for this season to transform a generation with words of wisdom from God and to empower the world for a radical experience for Jesus Christ. It has been an honor to know and experience a true servant of God with the heart of Christ."

Dr. Benjamin Stephens III, DMin
International Youth President, *Church of God in Christ*
Grandview, Missouri

"John, in his quest to deliver practical understanding of the Word of God, excavates the text for gems that others are afraid to discover."

Brianna Parker
Assimilation Director, *Friendship West Baptist Church*
Dallas, Texas

"As sure as the Christian will taste of the joys of life, it is inevitable that we will also taste of life's disappointments. It is in these times of disappointments that we must set our sights on our hope of glory in the midst of the storm. Starting with the Creation in Genesis, John Richards Jr. eloquently directs our focus toward Jesus Christ, the Creator, who is exalted in the culmination of Revelation. This thirty-day devotional won't keep you from the storms, but it will serve as a guide to give you rest through them!"

Brian Dye
Mentorship Director, *Grip Outreach For Youth*
Chicago, Illinois

"Transparent, authentic, honest, and empowering is how I would describe what we have in John's work. He isn't afraid to deal with the messiness of faith and ask the hard questions of God while helping us grow into a deeper relationship with God and those around us. This book has the power to change your life."

Dr. Ralph Basui Watkins, DMin, PhD
Associate Professor of Evangelism and Church Growth,
Columbia Theological Seminary
Atlanta, Georgia

About the Author

John C. Richards Jr. is the Associate Director of Adult Media Content at Urban Ministries, Inc., a Christian education content provider dedicated to providing quality material to churches worldwide. He oversees the development of the company's annual commentary and serves as the Developmental Editor of Urban Faith, a magazine for young Christian adults. John also serves as Managing Editor of UrbanFaith.com, an online platform with articles on faith and culture. The site garners over 9,000 unique views monthly.

John is an avid writer, whose blog, brotherpreacher.com, received the "Best-Faith Based Blog" award from the Black Weblog Awards in 2013. John's writing is witty, genuine, and transformative. A gifted public speaker, John has spoken at various conferences, churches, and events, touching on relationships, discipleship, spiritual disciplines, and faithfulness to Scripture. He received is BA from Morehouse college, his JD from Howard University School of Law, and his MDiv from Fuller Theological Seminary. He lives in Chicago, Illinois, with his wife, Sheridan, and their son, John III aka Scooter.

Contents

Introduction ... *xi*

Light ... *1*

Hoverer ... *5*

Transition ... *9*

Listening ... *13*

Lost ... *17*

Oil ... *21*

Silence ... *25*

Restoration ... *29*

Broken ... *33*

Desert ... *37*

Waiting ... *41*

Wilderness ... *45*

Exposed ... *49*

Touch ... *53*

Tears ... *57*

Obscurity ... *61*

Maestro 65

Between 69

Foxes. 73

Valley 77

Crucified 81

Encounter. 85

Mistakes. 89

Friday. 93

Look 97

Concealed 101

Adoption 105

Chains 109

Anger 113

Shine. 117

Introduction

I remember getting the call. I was on my way to preach a sermon for my homiletics class. Enrolled in seminary at the time, I looked forward to getting this sermon behind me. I thought preaching in a church was tough, but that's nothing compared to preaching in front of a dozen or so seminary students and a renowned homiletics professor. For some reason, this group seemed more intimidating than the hundred or so people who sat in a congregation on Sunday to hear me proclaim the Word of God.

But none of that mattered now. As a temporary California resident, I rarely got calls from my East Coast–embedded family this early in the morning. They normally respected the time difference and wouldn't call me until they were sure I was awake. As I groggily answered the phone just before dawn, my mother's words were muffled, yet discernable. *John, Daneé passed away this morning.*

The words hit me with hurricane-strength force. I bent over like a fragile palm tree, ready to break. Stuff like this isn't supposed to happen to me. I'm a Christian. I'm a seminary student. I love Jesus. I just spoke to Daneé on her birthday a few weeks ago. She was going to get dolled up. She had an appointment for a manicure and to get her eyebrows arched. I still remember how excited she was about going. And now she was gone. Just like that. No advanced notice. I had no time to prepare. Just an early morning phone call—a phone call that changed my life.

Daneé was my niece. She had a rare condition called aortic stenosis, a heart condition that impacted some of her other major organs. A week later I delivered my niece's eulogy. It only took one week for a new sermon to become the toughest sermon I ever preached. Nothing appears more insurmountable than eulogizing a loved one—especially one who died so young.

Sixteen years. One hundred ninety-two months. Eight hundred thirty-eight weeks. Five thousand eight hundred seventy-one days. Four surreal facts I used to begin my niece's eulogy. No three-point message would do. No preparation could remove the pain of those words. I had to comfort others as I processed my own pain. How do you exegete (a fancy theological word for explaining or critically interpreting a text) the death of a loved one? What kind of purpose could there be in death? How do you offer hope to others when you're on the verge of hopelessness?

We all experience loss. No matter our geographical location, we all travel there. Unlike trips to our favorite theme parks or favorite destination getaways, we don't look forward to visiting this place. Still, we visit when we least expect it. Our lives are good. Our family is good. Our career is good. Just when things couldn't get any better, we're booked on a one-way trip to Lossville.

Losing my niece wasn't my first trip to Lossville. In fact, I'd already had some frequent flyer miles built up. A year before then, I got a call the morning I sat for the Georgia Bar exam. My biological father had died. I didn't know my father too well. Strangely, the same brokenness I experienced losing my niece overwhelmed my soul. How could this be? How could I experience so much pain and despair over someone I barely knew? He showed up from time to time to bring me a gift when I was younger, but for the most part, he was as absent as a professional baseball player who'd been ejected from a game for breaking rules. My dad had struck out in major ways with me.

I tried my best to hold on to our relationship. I invited him to my high school graduation, hoping he'd be the proud father I always longed for. The day arrived. I walked across the stage, smiling from ear to ear, proud of my accomplishments. What a memorable night. In my mind, the night would end with me embracing my father in a moment made for Hallmark cards. But I searched for my dad. My eyes darted back and forth through the crowd. There was no sign of him.

After the ceremony, as the crowd began to disperse, it started to drizzle outside of my high school's quaint gymnasium. I was grateful for that drizzle. That way the tears that flooded my soul could be mistaken for raindrops—or maybe tears of joy. But there was pain in those tears—betrayal-laden tears. Once again, my father betrayed my trust. He took my trust and walked it to the curb like the disgruntled teen asked to drag garbage cans on trash day.

I lost a very close friend to breast cancer around the time of my dad's death. We were like two peas in a pod in high school—coordinating schedules to make sure we took classes together. She went on to get married and mother two handsome young men. When she died, she was only a few years past her thirtieth birthday—another unexpected trip to Lossville.

In retrospect, I can't imagine experiencing loss without simultaneously experiencing hope. That's the purpose of the pages that follow. I want to offer you the same hope I've experienced in my own loss and disappointment. And that hope is only found in one Person—Jesus Christ. This isn't some mystical, spiritual book on some "out there" force offering consolation, but words that I hope will confirm your need for the real, tangible presence of the Creator of the universe. I always tell others that the defense of my faith in Christ doesn't rest in arguing scriptural accuracy, but in the comfort I experience in trials and heartache. In these pages, I want you to feel that same comfort.

From the beginning to the end, the theme of hope is woven through Scripture. In its pages we confront men and women who deal with the same losses and disappointments we experience. We are presented with narratives of unbearable pain, death, childlessness, darkness, disease, brokenness, tears, and obscurity. Through this broken lens shines a glimmer of hope—Jesus Christ.

At some point in life, every Christian will experience loss, disappointment, and everything in between. Every Christian will board a flight to Lossville. But Lossville isn't our final destination. I want to offer you a glimpse of that destination. It's not a place, but a person—Jesus Christ, the hope of glory (Colossians 3:27). He is involved in God's redemptive story—from beginning to end. I pray that you see that in this devotional. The same hope I've experienced in my loss and disappointment is available for you today. No matter what loss you've experienced in your life, I offer you these words of consolation.

Day 1

Light

My wife and I hardly ever write checks when we pay bills. Given our penchant for using our debit cards almost exclusively, there are times when my check-writing skills are a bit rusty. But there are some things that still require us to pull out our tattered checkbook. And I've made the mistake of writing checks without noticing I've written them for the wrong amount. When I realize my error, I usually take out a large permanent marker and write "VOID" in corpulent letters across the check. That immediately makes the check worthless.

What happens when we move from paper voids to real tangible voids in our lives? What happens when there are permanent marks left on our lives that seem unfixable? What happens when those voids make our lives feel worthless? Loss of a job or a loved one can do just that. So it's no surprise that Scripture opens with God filling a void. If God is anything, he's a void-filler.

As the earth stood formless, dark, and void, we're given a glimpse of God's creation. As the Spirit of God hovered over the face of the waters, God pulled the curtain back on his creative studio and gave us an exclusive tour. He had so much to do. Trees needed to be planted. Mountains needed to be formed. Complex molecules needed to be combined to make up various elements. But what did he choose to do first? Speak light.

Think about that. Light was so critical to the story of Creation that it was the first thing God spoke. Even before humankind was created, God created light. Though humans were to be the apex of his creation, God felt the need to start with light. Maybe he created light first so that we'd know we were created to walk in light. Had he created us first, our only frame of reference would be darkness and we'd have to become accustomed to walking in light.

The writer of Romans mentions that we are without excuse for walking in this light, since God placed an understanding of his eternal power and divine nature in our hearts from the beginning (Romans 1:20). Creation is just a reflection of God thinking so highly of us that he uttered these words first: "Let there be light."

He purposely spoke light first. He wanted his people to experience light so we know and understand the Creator of that light. He wanted us to experience light so we know that darkness doesn't last always. He wanted us to experience light so we know that "light shines in darkness, and darkness has not overcome it" (John 1:5). Most of all, he wanted us to experience light so we may reflect that light.

But God still allows evenings, doesn't he? We experience them every day on our drives home from work as the sun disappears below the horizon. We also experience evenings as we travel along this road called "life." As long as the earth remains, there will be both day and night (Genesis 8:22). And night generates darkness. And darkness can be scary. That is, unless we realize that morning is right around the corner. And so is joy (Psalm 30:5). God allows our evenings to give us a greater appreciation of his light.

Is there anything as beautiful as the breaking of the day? There's something breathtaking about that moment. The same light that disappeared below the horizon and gave way to night peaks over the skyline, like a toddler trying to get a glimpse of a well-placed cookie jar on a kitchen counter. In that moment, light permeates our lives as we start a new day.

And we're reminded of the true light—the light that led the Israelites in the wilderness (Exodus 13:21). We're reminded of the light of the world—taking on flesh and dwelling among us (John 1:9, 14). His name? Jesus Christ. In whom we place all our hope. There's no void in our lives that he can't fill. In fact, all the other things we use to fill that void dissipate over time. They are temporal, false lights with a limited shelf life. But he is the true light—the hope of the world. He's the one who takes our seemingly worthless lives and ascribes ultimate value to them. So that in loss, in suffering, and in pain—whatever the darkness—his glorious light shines on our hearts (2 Corinthians 4:6).

> *God sees the voids in our lives. God sees the darkness in our lives. God sees our formlessness. The Spirit is there. He's hovering. Just waiting for God to speak those timeless words. That's when God enters our stories and says, "Let there be light." So wherever you are today, know that God is pursuing you. Even as darkness and voids surround you, he's there. To offer you hope. With four simple, yet penetrating words. Let. There. Be. Light.*

"And God said, 'Let there be light,' and there was light." (Genesis 1:3)

DAY 2

Hoverer

Having five siblings can teach you a lot of life lessons. Among those lessons is the practice of hovering. At this point in my life, I consider myself a professional "hoverer." I can hover with the best of them.

Let me explain the nature of a hoverer. A hoverer is one who waits in anticipation to take advantage of a great opportunity. All they need to proceed? They just need to hear a word. Friday nights in my household I became that person. Reluctant to cook after a long week, my mother would bring home takeout. As soon as she walked in the house, my hands were washed and I was ready. I was so close to the food I could breathe in its fresh aroma. I stood near her, just hovering, until I heard the words: "Go ahead. Dig in."

The Bible makes mention of another Hoverer. He might be considered the greatest Hoverer ever. One whose proverbial sandal I am not able to strap. He didn't hover over food. He wasn't trying to satisfy his appetite, just the unfolding plan of the Creator. And his situation wasn't as highly aromatic as mine. In fact, here are a few words that describe his environment: disorderly, chaotic, and hopeless. Three excellent descriptions of the early appearance of the landmass we have come to know as earth. There were no awe-inspiring mountains yet. There were no rushing rivers. More importantly, there was no ability to sustain human life.

The earth didn't have a chance. Yet the Spirit of God was present. Hovering. He was merely waiting for the go-ahead from the Father. There's a sense of anticipation as he waits to hear those words: "Let there be light" (Genesis 1:3). It's like God says, "Go ahead. Dig in." That was his cue. It was time to turn this chaos into order. It was time to replace darkness with light. It was time to turn an abyss into a place of bliss. Six days later the results were awe-inspiring. So beautiful that the Father sat back and declared it all "very good" (Genesis 1:31).

Ultimately this story finds its way into our own hearts. Although formed and not created, humankind can be described in the same way: disorderly, chaotic, and hopeless. At one point in my life, those terms described me with succinct accuracy. But there was a Hoverer present. The Spirit of God was waiting to hear those words from the Father: "Go ahead. Dig in." And did he ever! He breathed on me. I was like the earth—a life devoid of the presence of God.

Yet the Spirit was hovering. And something amazing happened. Minerals began to appear, creating salt (Matthew

5:13). Darkness began to fade, disseminating light (Matthew 5:16). Rivers of living water began to flow out of my life (John 7:38). And my heart began to change.

> *Paul reminds us all of that day in a letter to the church at Corinth: "For God, who said, 'Let light shine out of darkness,' has shone in our hearts to give the light of the knowledge of the glory of God in the face of Jesus Christ" (2 Corinthians 4:6). Not only are the opening verses of Genesis about the earth's creation, but also your heart's recreation through grace. Today, be grateful for God invading your world and "digging in." Be grateful for the Great Hoverer, the Spirit of God. Continue to allow him to breathe on you. And as you do, trust me, the Father sits back and declares those timeless words: "Very good!"*

"The earth was without form and void, and darkness was over the face of the deep. And the Spirit of God was hovering over the face of the waters." (Genesis 1:2)

Day 3

Transition

Have you ever moved before? Moving is one of those experiences that is both exciting and fearful. It's very easy to be excited about moving. You get to experience new places, new people, and new things. On the other hand, moving can be very taxing.

There are some things that are characteristic of every move. We sit there surrounded by boxes wondering how things will ever get done. Some of us are perfect planners, so we get all packed weeks in advanced. But others wait until the absolute last minute to get everything done. So two days before the move we find ourselves standing there—overwhelmed—packing tape on one hip, a pair of scissors in hand, and a stack of newspapers sitting at our feet. We realize that it has to be done in order for us to move. That's the only way we'll be able to transition.

Life's transitions can be just as exciting and taxing, can't they? We realize this thing called life has to be done. We have to move forward. We can't buy back lost time. We can't go back. But we look around and exasperatingly declare, "How in the world am I going to deal with this?" Instead of looking around and seeing boxes, tape, and scissors, we're surrounded by uncertainty, fear, and unpredictability. It's reassuring that men and women in Scripture had some of the same problems.

I'm pretty sure when Abram was called to leave his family and everything else familiar to him, he experienced some level of excitement (Genesis 12). What kind of new things did God have in store for him? He heard God tell him to leave everything and go to another land. A new land. A place where he could experience new cuisine and new attractions. But it would be a taxing journey. In leaving his father's house, he was in essence giving up the inheritance he was guaranteed from his father (Hebrews 11:8). The opulent lifestyle, the lavish land, and the respected title were gone in one fell swoop. But he left.

Here's something you need to know about Abram. God never gave him one detail about his journey. Not even a small hint as to where he was going. He's left all this security without a roadmap to his eventual destination. What God does tell him seems cryptic. "Go...to the land that I will show you" (Genesis12:1). *That's it. A land that I will show you? Awesome. Thanks a lot, God.* For detail-oriented people like myself, that's nerve-racking.

Transition teaches you something, though. Faith is truly the evidence of things not seen (Hebrews 11:1) In transition we experience a lot of things we aren't able to see. Finding a job can be rough. But we are asked to have faith. Finding any form of normalcy can be rough. Be we are asked to have faith. Finding a church home can be rough. But we are asked to have faith. Transition requires faith. Without it, any transition in our life is doomed.

Abram's call was familiar to his family member. His father, Terah, had taken his family from Ur of the Chaldeans to make their way to Canaan. But they found themselves settling in Haran (Genesis 11:31). They never made it to Canaan. Maybe their faith waned. For them, settling was far easier than pressing forward. They'd forgotten the call.

Even though there are times where God doesn't give us details about our transition, we should always remember and celebrate the call—having faith that God will see us through. Having faith that he finishes the work that he starts in us (Philippians 1:6). Having faith that he does this work through his Son, Jesus Christ. The same Christ who is before all things and in all things, who holds all things together (Colossians 1:17), holds our lives together. Wrap your transition in that truth. Pack your fears away in that reality. And God's peace will guard your heart and mind (Philippians 4:7).

God would never have called Abram if he didn't already know where the land was he would show him. Even if you can't see it, God knows the answer to all the normal questions: Who? What? When? Where? How? Why? Celebrate God's faithfulness in the midst of your uncertainty. That's grace—tenacious grace. A grace that shows God's continual provision for you and shows you he's walking by your side. So, go already. You'll be amazed how God honors your obedience with his sustenance.

"And I am sure of this, that he who began a good work in you will bring it to completion at the day of Jesus Christ." (Philippians 1:6)

Day 4

Listening

Dysfunctional households can detrimentally impact our lives. There are countless stories of men and women who grew up in troubling environments. Men and women whose stories move far beyond that embarrassing drunk uncle they hated seeing at family reunions. Instead, their stories plunge them into the choppy waters of abuse, neglect, and inhabitable conditions. Like badges of shame, they carry the scars into their adult lives. They refuse to trust others because of past betrayal. They refuse to get close to anyone because of past abandonment or absenteeism. Whatever the case, dysfunction can rob us of our hope.

Ishmael's story is the definition of dysfunction. An afterthought, he owed his existence to Sarai's inability to bear children. Ishmael was the backup plan. He was Plan B. He was Mr. "Just In Case." Abram and Sarai were barren, unable to have children. Otherwise, we wouldn't know Ishmael's story. Sarai came up with a plan. *Take my servant and have a baby with her.* As present-day readers, we know this is asking for trouble (you don't just invite another person into your marriage). But she wanted to see her husband happy (Genesis 16:1–3).

Ishmael's mother, Hagar, was just being obedient by bearing a child for a barren couple, at her master's request. Little did she know that this would cause Sarai to resent her and regret that Ishmael was ever born (Genesis 16:4). Then it happened. Sarai had her own child. She'd made her husband happy. She had no more use for this young boy. Hagar and Ishmael were exiled (Genesis 21:9–21). But God heard their cries.

Ishmael's name means"God hears," but his life up until this point was anything but God hearing. Imagine that. He was always considered "that slave woman's child." His own father sent him away to die, with just bread and water (a nice inheritance, right?). God hears? Yeah, right!

The young lad sat nearby as his mother wept over their impending death. His mother had reached the end of her rope. Ishmael's life was almost over before God heard. He was in a dry place before God heard. He was severely malnourished before God heard. But God heard.

As Christians we have confidence that God hears us too. In Scripture we're told that if we ask anything according to his will, he hears us (1 John 5:14). He hears our cries (Psalm 34:17). But let's be honest. We might find ourselves in Ishmael's place before then, feeling ostracized and abandoned. Dysfunction might characterize our past, but God hears.

Ishmael never rejoined his dysfunctional family. He went on to start his own family, never to be a part of Abraham's immediate household again. If you ask him, he didn't ask for the dysfunction. He may have wanted a relationship with his father. He may have wanted to spend his days hanging out with his half-brother Isaac. But God, who was listening, worked through the dysfunction and promised to make Ishmael a great nation (Genesis 21:18).

God is listening. He may not give you the solution you want, but he will give you the solution you need. Whatever trial you've encountered over the past week, the past month, or past year, walk in the assurance that God hears. You have been adopted into the family of God. You are a joint heir with Jesus (Romans 8:17). It might be dry right now. You might feel like somebody's backup plan. You may feel malnourished but rest in the hope that God hears.

"In the day of my trouble I call upon you, for you answer me." (Psalm 86:7)

Day 5

Lost

Have you ever lost anything? Despair and hopelessness enter the scene when something is lost. I've torn my home to shreds looking for items I've lost. I've scoured my "everything drawer" looking for the one cord I need to plug in an electronic device. I've looked through my closet for my favorite shirt—the one I wanted to wear to a formal event. Cord, shirt, or anything else, I'm inconsolable until I find that item.

My son experienced this on a much smaller scale recently. He loves fruit snacks. I'd say they are his favorite snack. One day, after picking him up from school, I gave him a pack to enjoy. He was primed and ready to have a party in his mouth. But then the unthinkable happened. He dropped one fruit snack, and it rolled underneath the seat. You would have thought he just found out his best friend was moving across the country. The tears began to flow, and he became a small-model Niagara Falls in the back of the car. Here's the crazy part. A bunch of fruit snacks were still in the bag, but he was focused on the one that fell under the seat. He should have realized that daddy was still in the car. Daddy was still in control. Daddy was still driving. And that's all that really mattered.

Our experiences in life can get just like this. God straps us in, gets us ready for our journey, and blesses us with many great things to enjoy in this life. Then the unthinkable happens. We lose one of those things. It falls out of sight. And we're distraught. That thing would have brought us joy. That thing would have satisfied us. And we forget this simple fact: Daddy is still in the car. And that's all that really matters. If we aren't careful, we can subtly desire things more than we desire God. This is most telling in our reaction to losing those things.

In the Gospels, Jesus' most frequently quoted saying deals with losing. "Whoever seeks to preserve his life will lose it, but whoever loses his life will keep it" (Luke 17:33). In Luke's gospel, he prefaces this by saying, "Remember Lot's wife" (Luke 17:32).

Lot's wife is mentioned once in Scripture. She's not even mentioned by name. Why would Jesus tell us to remember Lot's wife? The story is familiar to us all. As Lot and his family are fleeing Sodom's judgment, his wife looks back and is turned into a pillar of salt (Genesis 19:26).

She obviously had some affection for the city she was fleeing. She wanted to get one last look—one last taste of what it felt like to live in Sodom. Her legs were moving in one direction, but her heart was being tugged in another. She couldn't stand the thought of losing something so dear. Her fruit snack had fallen.

We look at the story of Lot's wife today and ask why she was so foolish. She'd been warned not to look back. Why would she do such a thing? The harsh truth is that it is easy to look back.

Our Sodom might be different, but if we lose something that grips our hearts without replacing it with the One who fills the void, we are in danger of going back to that very thing. Pastor and author Tim Keller calls this process recognizing the idol, renouncing the idol, and replacing the idol. Until you've done all three, you'll begin to long for the thing you think you've lost—the thing you think brought you fulfillment. And the idol reclaims the throne of your heart. Just ask Lot's wife.

It wasn't until I began losing stuff that I began to find true satisfaction in my life in Christ Jesus. Paul knew this and declared, "I have been crucified with Christ. It is no longer I who live, but Christ lives in me. And the life I now live in the flesh I live by faith in the Son of God, who loved me and gave himself for me" (Galatians 2:20). Losing stuff isn't necessarily a bad thing. It's just that you need to replace it with something—or, in our case, Someone. That's what my son was missing that day in the car. His daddy had so much more for him. Much more than he could think or imagine.

And that's your Father's promise to us today. Don't lose hope. Don't despair. There's a time to lose (Ecclesiastes 3:6). Losing anything for Christ's sake is far better than anything in this temporal life. Because in losing, you gain eternal life.

"Whoever finds his life shall lose it, and whoever loses his life for my sake shall find it." (Matthew 10:39)

Day 6

Oil

My mother used to keep a ubiquitous pot on our stove. It was a black, cast-iron pot that housed one of the hottest commodities in our house: Crisco. Crisco used to come in this large can that looked like a lard-filled block when opened. Whenever my mother needed to fry something, she'd break out that can of Crisco and throw some in a pot. The heat would melt it and cause it to liquefy. That was the sign. It was time to get cooking. Once she was done cooking, my mother didn't throw the oil out. She'd drain it, remove all the debris, and retain the good oil for future use. That pot remained on the stove until the next time she prepared to fry a southern delicacy. My mother realized one thing that I've learned over the years as a Christian: don't ever lose your oil.

You never know when your voice will be heard. You can spend years ministering in a virtual abyss. The amens are sparse. The blog traffic is hit and miss. There are other voices out there saturating the market. Quality gives way to quantity. But you labor along.

David knows exactly how you feel. He was the shepherd in the back hills of Israel tending to his flock. Waiting to be anointed and given regal authority, yet uninvited. Almost forgotten. Laboring away in the fields while the prophet is in town looking for someone after God's heart.

He makes his way home. As he approaches, he realizes there is a celebration. Had he forgotten one of his sibling's birthdays? He browsed his mental calendar, eliminating each one by one, not knowing that another elimination ceremony was taking place as he plodded his way through the grassy knoll that sustained his flocks.

He crossed the threshold of his home, simultaneously crossing the threshold of his future. There was no time to shower. He smelled like a shepherd—a sweet savor when God is looking for a shepherd king. It "reeked" of humility—the willingness to labor for the vulnerable and protect those who are susceptible. After a few missed calls, the prophet recognized David at once. He broke open his anointing oil. The aroma saturated the room. It was an alabaster box moment. The oil was costly, but David had also paid a price. The cost? Anonymity. It was now his time.

Shepherd and king meet in this moment, but the next day he didn't find himself on a throne. He found himself again out to pasture. He found himself back in Faithful

Over the Few University. Class was back in session. He was anointed but not disappointed.

Did you find yourself in that story? You might not be tending sheep, but you've been laboring in obscurity. Looking for a bit of hope. You'd perused the worn pages of your study Bible. Highlighted, wept over, and meditated on, the text has prepared you for your return to "shepherding" with knowledge that you are royalty. All things work together for the good of those who love him (Romans 8:28).

While it is true that the gifting and calling of God are irrevocable, you may find yourself meandering along in relative unimportance until you are trustable. Until you reach a point where your ability is supplanted by God's ability—a point where your trainability becomes God's sustainability. Where your heart stops confessing I am not able and starts declaring God is able. That's where hope resides—in God's ability to see you through. King David had reached that point. His brothers seemed more qualified. He didn't know how he would move from shepherd's staff to king's scepter. But then he took a deep breath.

Inhale.

Exhale.

The oil was still there. Even when it seemed depleted. When the flock's numbers vacillated, it was there. On the cold, starry nights, it was there. The presence of the oil constantly reminding David, You are a king.

> *In your season of waiting, be patient. Take a deep breath. Inhale. Exhale. It's still there. God's still there. Guiding you. Consoling you. Shaping you. Whatever you do, brother and sister, don't lose your oil.*

"You have loved righteousness and hated wickedness. Therefore God, your God, has anointed you with the oil of gladness beyond your companions." (Psalm 45:7)

Day 7

Silence

There's some level of discomfort when things are silent. Maybe it's because culture fills our lives with so much noise. We Facebook. We tweet. We browse. We text. We hashtag. I don't feel like I'm being productive unless I'm doing about forty-five things at once. The amount of tabs and windows I have open on my computer right now—about fifteen—is indicative of this innate desire to busy ourselves. Busying ourselves gives us the chance to avoid silence. Silence is uncomfortable. Silence is discouraging, especially when that silence comes from the God of the universe.

But it happens, doesn't it? Ask Elijah. He was riding a spiritual high. He'd just won a convincing victory in a battle with the prophets of Baal. God had shown up. Elijah had spent three-and-a-half years of ministry doing great deeds and experiencing God's protection. But it took one threat from Jezebel to change all of that. She'd heard what he did to the prophets at Carmel and vowed to spend all her energy trying to take Elijah's life (1 Kings 19:1–2).

And Elijah ran—a victor one moment, a coward the

next. He made his way to Bersheeba, a region known for its unpredictable climate and dryness. Trials tend to do that to us too. We flee. We get away. And go to unpredictable places. Dry places. Our conditions cause us to cast aside past victories like used paper towels. And we find ourselves in a rut.

But Bersheeba wasn't enough for Elijah. The threat was so severe that Elijah decided to go further into the wilderness. He left his servant at Bersheeba (1 Kings 19:3). He'd given up on himself. No need for him to bring someone else down in his misery, right? He'd deal with this alone. Things got so bad that Elijah wished he were dead (1 Kings 19:4). Little did he know, he was headed for an encounter with God.

Elijah vacillated between wanting to live one day and wanting to die another. He left because of the threat of death; now he just wanted to die. Think about that. Elijah, the great prophet, struggled with life and death. In his narrative, we're reminded that Elijah is a man just like us (James 5:17).

As I write this, over the past two months there have been reports of three pastors who have committed suicide. On the surface, they had perfect lives but were eaten alive by their trials. They preached people happy on Sundays, but they were unhappy themselves. People expected them to be more than what they really were—mere men. Men with struggles, pains, and heartaches who may have covered them to keep up the perfect appearance expected of them.

But Elijah would have none of this. He wore his humanity on his chest. He went to the one place he knew he could find comfort. He traveled for another 40 days in this wilderness, ultimately making his way to Mount Horeb—the same mountain where Moses experienced the burning bush and the passing presence of God (Exodus 3; 33). *If I can just get to the mountain,* he thought. But what he found on the mountain wasn't what he expected. He got silence.

Here was a prophet who has seen the fire of God fall from heaven and devour an altar. He was used to God doing things on a grand scale. He was anticipating something big. Not this time. There was wind. There was an earthquake. There was fire. But God wasn't in any of it. Elijah found his hope in the sound of a low whisper (1 Kings 19:12). God's message to Elijah—and to us—is that miracles and signs are great, but what he needed in that moment was God's Word. That's what was going to sustain him in his trial.

At times our stories mirror Elijah's. Things can get just as bad for us. Trials come out of nowhere. All it takes is one phone call. One text. One conversation. And things go haywire. And as they go haywire, God seems to be silent.

But God says the same thing to us that he says to Elijah in his experience: *I'm working...even in the silence.*

> *Moses and Elijah both meet God on this mountain. But they'll later meet on another mountain (Matthew 17:1–3). There they'll meet Jesus, the true object of their hope. There's no fire. There's no wind. There's no earthquake. Just the Word of God—made flesh. Just as the disciples are getting ready to build tabernacles for Jesus and the two prophets, God speaks. "This is my beloved son...listen to him" (Matthew 17:5). Today, I leave you with those same words. Whatever the trial, listen to him. He's working for you, even in the silence.*

"Be still and know that I am God. I will be exalted among the nations, I will be exalted in the earth!" (Psalm 46:10a)

Day 8

Restoration

The death of a spouse can shatter a widower's world, like a piece of glass pelted with rocks by mischievous juveniles. Ask anyone who has lost a spouse and they'll tell you as much. All they've known for as long as they've been married has been tied to their spouse. The way the house is organized reminds them of their significant other. Watching certain movies brings to mind the quiet moments they shared together on the couch. Driving by a frequented dining spot brings to mind certain sounds, sights, and tastes. It is gut-wrenching to write about this topic. I can't imagine losing my wife. She's such an integral part of my life. For many, losing a spouse is a bitter reality. A tough pill to swallow, even for Christians.

Naomi knew all about this. She'd traveled with her husband, Elimelech, to Moab. There was a famine in Bethlehem. Ironically, Bethlehem means "house of bread." But there was no bread in the house. So they set out with the expectation that their hope would be restored in Moab, where there seemed to be plenty of food. But Elimelech died during their stint in Moab (Ruth 1:1–3).

Naomi spent the next ten years in Moab, grieving the loss of her husband. Her sons took wives from the land and things were starting to stabilize for her. But then the unspeakable happened. Both her sons died. Naomi was devastated. She's left there in Moab. All the men in her life were now taken from her. I can hear Naomi's lament now. *How could this happen? Why, oh Lord?*

And there she stands with her two daughters-in-law—grieving. And in her grief, she tries to offer her daughters-in-law some hope. *I don't have anything else to give you. My sons are gone. There's nothing I can do for you. Go home. I'm hopeless.* Can you blame her? Ten years. No grandbabies—because you know grandmothers love them some grandbabies. She has no hope of a male heir. As a widow, she'd now be economically dependent on the social structures around her. So she looks to release her daughters-in-law from any obligation to her. One of them, Orpah, heeds her call and leaves. The other, Ruth, sticks with Naomi. Orpah left. Ruth stayed. Orpah lost hope. Ruth retained it, grasping it like a hungry infant indulging in the first few moments of a meal. What was the difference?

Ruth, a Moabite, had encountered a god that she hadn't experienced before. Naomi's God, the God of Israel, was now her God. There was no way she was turning back. He offered hope unlike any other. Maybe it was the way she saw Naomi handle her suffering. After losing a husband and two children, Naomi now wanted to return to her homeland because "the Lord had visited his people" (Ruth 1:6). Though Naomi's hope was waning, she trusted that the same God who visited her homeland would visit her again. Ruth saw this glimmer of hope in Naomi. And she clung to her.

In returning to Bethlehem with Naomi, Ruth meets a relative of her father-in-law, Boaz. Boaz becomes her redeemer—as was custom at this time—and marries Ruth. And what happens to Naomi? Her hope is fully restored. Ruth has a child. Naomi becomes the child's nurse. A grandbaby. A male heir. Her hope fully restored.

How do you suffer well? How do you retain hope in the midst of pain, heartache, and sorrow? Keep in mind that the Lord has visited his people. The greater Boaz has entered our story and redeemed us. His name is Jesus Christ. Immanuel. God with us. There is bread in the house again. He is the bread of life (John 6:35). Stand on that promise. Give all your pain, heartache, and sorrow to the Redeemer. He will restore you.

"For I know that my Redeemer lives, and at last he will stand upon the earth." (Job 19:25)

Day 9

Broken

Potters have expectations when working with clay. They expect high temperatures to induce reactions that lead to permanent changes in the clay. This includes an increase in strength and the setting of their shapes.

Jeremiah uses potter and clay language to speak of God's relationship with us. He tells us that the clay was marred in the hand of the potter (Jeremiah 18:1–4). Doesn't that sound painful? Why would a loving God want to do that to us?

I've spent a lot of time in my life feeling marred and out of shape. *God, is this really what you want me to be? A whole clump of clay, without shape?* I had a lack of direction. Not only did I feel marred, but things began to heat up around me. I started getting a little more irritable at home. I started to be short with people I normally put up with.

Things heat up for us all, don't they? There's hopelessness in the heat, isn't there? But God shapes us in the high temperatures in our lives. It's impossible for clay to be shaped without high temperatures. Pottery must be fired to a temperature high enough to mature the clay. No heat, no maturity. It's the same with life. Maturity only happens when things get hot. Clay that is not heated cracks and breaks. It's easier to work with clay that is heated. Are you feeling the heat in your life? Maybe, just maybe, the potter is at work. Are you moldable? Becoming a follower of Jesus doesn't remove our trials. Ask Paul. He encouraged the church at Rome to glory in their trials (Romans 5:3).

One of the most crucial tools in the potter's life is his wheel. The wheel is made to revolve rapidly while the clay under construction is pressed, squeezed, and pulled gently into shape. The wheel (will) of God is the same way. While we are revolving in life, we are pressed, squeezed, and pulled by our daily circumstances. Why? For the potter, this usually happens because the clay might contain a hidden impurity—a flaw beneath the surface. It's no different with our Potter. There are times when we think we have it all together. But God has to step in and reveal a hidden impurity, a flaw beneath the surface.

Are you being pressed, squeezed, or pulled in life? Maybe there is something hidden that God is trying to get at. He wants you in your purest form. The clay on the wheel is also pressed because there are times when it is stiff and unyielding. Like the clay, we can be stiff and unyielding. *God, you want me to do what? You want me to go where? Are you sure about that?* We don't want to budge an inch. But the pressing and squeezing gets us to a place of obedience and submission to the Potter's shaping.

Finally, the Potter's most basic tools are his hands. There aren't many people today whose basic tools are their hands. Artists join potters in this unique class of individuals. In those occupations, handwork is slow. But this handwork offers the potter a high degree of control over the shaping of the clay. And the handwork allows potters to use their imaginations to create one-of-a-kind works of art.

> *Aren't there times when you feel like something was taking forever to happen? Remember, the Potter takes his time. God does this to create a "one-of-a-kind" work of art. Did you know that you were a one-of-a-kind? Fearfully and wonderfully made? God doesn't want to duplicate anyone or anything else in your life. Paul says that we are "(God's) workmanship" (Ephesians 2:10). Let the Potter take his time with you.*

"I praise you, for I am fearfully and wonderfully made. Wonderful are your works; my soul knows it very well." (Psalm 139:14)

Day 10

Desert

When I lived in Los Angeles, it seemed like there was always some kind of construction going on. New buildings were going up almost weekly. New routes were planned, bulldozed, and built to accommodate this expansion. One particular construction site was intriguing. The construction crew was building a highway extension on a piece of land that cars weren't able to navigate before. The crew didn't have to worry about any obstacles, since the land was barren. The best new construction usually takes place on barren land.

What about when things get barren in our lives? When the tumbleweeds of worry and concern begin to roll through our lives? How might these deserts bring us hope? There's a desert in Scripture that might just do that.

Four hundred plus years. That's how long the Jewish people waited. Between Malachi and Matthew, God spoke very little—at least publicly. Finally, the Word of God came to John in the wilderness (Matthew 3:1–3). What happened during that four centuries of silence? Why had God not spoken during that time? There were still prophets around. There were still priests around, right? But all they heard was silence.

The closing words from the book of Malachi were hanging in the balance. "Behold, I will send you Elijah the prophet before the great and awesome day of the Lord comes. And he will turn the hearts of fathers to their children and the hearts of children to their fathers..." (Malachi 4:5–6).

And how did God decide to break the silence? Did he show up in the synagogue? Did he show up at the top of the Temple mount? No. He spoke to a man who wore a leather belt and ate locusts—a man who came forward in the spirit of the prophet Elijah to declare a baptism of repentance. A man named John the Baptist. A crazy prophet who shows up in the most unorthodox place—a desert. Proclaiming the Word of the Lord in a desert? That's a horrible church growth model.

The Jewish people had been experiencing a spiritual drought. They were subjected to Roman empirical rule, a far cry from the great nation God told Abraham he would bless way back in Genesis. The last place most of them wanted to go in a spiritual drought was to a desert. *I'm already spiritually dry; don't ask me to go out to a desert.* But that's where God chose to deliver his message—in a desert.

The Jewish people had to be willing to leave a spiritual desert to enter a physical desert. That's a tall order, isn't it? But these devout people of the Book also knew the words of Isaiah. "A voice cries: 'In the wilderness prepare the way of the Lord; make straight in the desert a highway for our God'" (Isaiah 40:3). That's right. The Lord's way would be prepared in the desert. That's the paradox of God's kingdom. It takes a desert to end a drought.

We go through spiritual droughts in our life, don't we? The sermons just aren't doing it for us. The worship team isn't singing our favorite songs. Our favorite podcast pastor is doing a series on the state of his church that's completely irrelevant to us 3,000 miles away. The drought is real. It's palpable. And then we come to this passage. And we're told that God is speaking in the desert. And we scratch our heads. We aren't trying to go through a drought. It hurts. It's dry. It's unnerving. *Why not speak in a nice hotel room in Miami? Why not speak on a Caribbean getaway vacation?* The Isaiah passage gives us a hint.

Isaiah says to make a highway in the desert for our God. A highway? In the desert? Like that construction crew I noticed in Los Angeles, God rarely builds a highway on top of roads we've already traveled. When you experience spiritual droughts, there may be some unexplored areas God may be trying to take you. You haven't traveled them before. It's new construction. But, in the end, it will make your journey easier.

We also can't expect God to build on top of something that has already been built. That's one of the mistakes we can make when we lose hope. Like the builders of the Tower of Babel, we start to build things to inspire ourselves, exalt ourselves, and reassure ourselves. But our hope lies in our reliance on the Great Builder. The One who takes our droughts and gives us direction.

> *Deserts are very real in the life of Christians. They are unavoidable, yet necessary. It's in the desert that you should turn to the Source. You should turn to Jesus Christ, the One who gives living water (John 7:37–38). He is the One who provides an oasis for our souls. Today, see your drought as an opportunity to encounter Christ.*

"On the last day of the feast, the great day, Jesus stood up and cried out, "If anyone thirsts, let him come to me and drink. Whoever believes in me, as the Scripture has said, 'Out of his heart will flow rivers of living water.'" (John 7:37–38)

Day 11

Waiting

Growing up in the Baptist church, words like "Advent" and "Lent" were foreign to me. Attending seminary many years after becoming a Christian is what exposed me to their meanings. I discovered there was an Advent season that led up to Christmas. This season was a special time of waiting. Derived from the Latin term *adventus,* meaning "coming," Advent is when many Christians spend four weeks before Christmas in eager anticipation of the date when they celebrate Jesus' birth. It's a time of reflection. It's a time of self-reflection. Most of all, it's a time of waiting.

Every Christmas season we send out Hallmark cards that communicate a peaceful, orderly, serene, quiet manger scene with Joseph and Mary. Animals, kings, and shepherds surround them as they gaze upon Jesus, the Savior of the world. The same Jesus they'd been waiting on. But peace, order, and serenity wouldn't have been the words Joseph used to describe his waiting. He'd just traveled eighty miles from Nazareth to Bethlehem with a very pregnant wife to be counted in a census. Upon arrival, they were told that there was no room for them in the local inn (Luke 2:1–7).

Several months prior, Mary told Joseph something you don't want to hear as a fiancé. She sat him down on the couch, grasped his hands gently, and quietly stated, "I'm pregnant." Joseph jumped up in disbelief. As her fiancé, he hadn't so much come near her. Not even a kiss. In fact, after their betrothal, as is custom, Mary went back to live with her family and was to remain there until they were officially married. The marriage had not yet been consummated. And Joseph, being a righteous man, did everything in his power to keep their relationship pure until they were married. Pregnant? How can this be? Joseph found himself waiting.

Scripture doesn't tell us how long it was before an angel appeared to Joseph in a dream to tell him that Mary's pregnancy was an act of the creative power of the Holy Spirit. In fact, we're told that Joseph was trying to find a way to divorce her quietly (Matthew 1:19). He spent a significant amount of time waiting. Contemplating his decision.

We wait too, don't we? We wait for answers to prayers. Hearts racing, we sit in hospital lobbies and wait for news from doctors. We wait. Since waiting is a reservoir for doubt, all kinds of thoughts run through our minds. *I don't know if I can stomach being disappointed again. What if they don't pull through? Did I miss God on this one?*

As he waited, Joseph was reminded that there are times where God delivers you in the way that you need and not necessarily the way that you want. When Mary told him the news, I'm pretty sure that Joseph just wanted to wash his hands of the situation. I'm pretty sure he was right on the verge of issuing that certificate of divorce to his would-be wife. That would have been easier for him to deal with. It would have been less messy that way. Just then, the angel showed up with this message: what has been conceived in your wife is from the Holy Spirit. You'll call him Jesus, because he will deliver his people from their sins. Matthew's gospel goes on to say that this was done in order to fulfill an ancient prophecy in Isaiah: the virgin will be with child and will give birth to a son, and they will call him Immanuel—which means, "God with us." Joseph's waiting became "Immanuel" (Matthew 1:20–22).

God with us. Jesus would fulfill that role over the next thirty-three years of his life, but the Jewish people wouldn't quite understand his purpose. They were looking for a Messiah who would lead a revolt and overthrow the Roman government. Insurrection was on their minds. But this wasn't on Jesus' agenda. He had an agenda: a bloody death as a remission for our sins. "This cup that is poured out for you is the new covenant in my blood" (Luke 22:20).

Through Jesus, God had delivered his people in the way that they needed. Yes, they needed a king, but they were desperately in need of a Savior. It wasn't what they wanted. But it was precisely what they needed. I can hear

God saying, "My thoughts are not your thoughts, neither are your ways my ways" (Isaiah 55:8).

Waiting often causes us to believe that we know precisely what we need to deliver us. We rebel. We want to overthrow things God has established in our lives. Sometimes we get so desperate we feel spiritual bondage. We want to wash our hands of the things that trouble us. We want to walk away.

But God has provided another way—a way that we might not quite understand. A way that seems to be contrary to everything we understand about our future. And his first moments were spent in a stable in Bethlehem. His infant lungs taking their first breath in anticipation of his final breath on the cross. Good news wrapped in swaddling clothes. Good news we all need every moment of our lives.

Can you stop allowing your waiting to dictate your actions and allow Jesus to be Immanuel? A God who will never leave you or forsake you. A God who knows what you need before you even ask. A God who has you covered through the redemptive power of his cross.

."And now, O Lord, for what do I wait? My hope is in you." (Psalm 39:7)

Day 12

Wilderness

I love God's sense of humor. When I married my wife, she had a few non-negotiable items. I'll share one of them with you. *Whatever you do, don't ask me to move to Michigan* (sorry, Michiganders). I'm licensed to practice law in Michigan and spent a few years there, so just in case I was thinking about a return, she shut that down like lights coming on at a house party. I can't blame her. My wife is a Southern California girl. She likes perfect eighty-degree weather, sundresses, and lattes—okay, she's not the latte type, but you get my point.

Fast forward several years and we now live in Chicago, Illinois. I'd been offered a job with a company in Chicago. Months later, my wife interviewed for and accepted a position as an executive director of a non-profit Christian summer camp. Here's the kicker. The camp was in Michigan. Driving to the camp for the first time after she was hired, I remember asking her, *do you remember what you told me when we got married?* We shared a chuckle. As we drove toward the camp, I realized one thing: the camp was rural.

My wife's call had literally led her to the wilderness. And I believed she was in good company.

The Father had just affirmed Jesus. The voice boomed from heaven. "You are my beloved Son" (Mark 1:11). Not just any son, but God's Beloved Son. What a moment that must have been for Jesus. There are inner city kids today who would love to hear those words. Growing up without my biological father, I understand what fatherless inner city kids feel when it comes to hearing those words. And in some sense, Jesus does too. Scripture records this affirmation for the first time when Jesus is about thirty years old. Imagine spending years hearing whispers that you're a child of a couple that wasn't even married when you were born (Matthew 1:18–24). Imagine the questions that arose when Mary told her loved ones that her child was a miracle of God. I'm sure Jesus heard these whispers. But on this day, he didn't hear a whisper. The heavens shook. And his Father spoke.

After such a monumental moment, Jesus started healing people and performing various signs immediately, right? Nope. He found himself in the wilderness for forty days (Mark 1:13). Tempted by Satan. Hanging around with wild animals and angels. This isn't what ministry was supposed to look like. But there he was. Called to the wilderness. Make no mistake about it, if you are called of God, wilderness awaits. It might not be a rural camp in Michigan, but some form of wilderness will accompany your call. It's where you're tested. It's where your character is developed. Most of all, it's where God gets the glory.

God doesn't leave us in our wilderness alone. There are a few things that have comforted me in the wilderness. First, there is comfort in knowing that there's a driver. I got my license when I was sixteen years old. Without fail, since that time I'm always the designated driver. I feel like I have a sign on my chest that reads, "Ask me, I'll drive." No matter where, or with whom, when there's a road trip I'm asked to drive. Here's something my passengers realize. Getting me to drive relieves stress and takes the pressure off of them to get us to our destination.

Mark's gospel tells us that the Spirit of God drove Jesus into the wilderness. He didn't lead him. He didn't nudge him. He didn't guide him. He drove him. And when the Spirit drives, the passenger thrives. Allowing the Spirit to lead you takes the pressure off and relieves you of the stress of trying to navigate through life.

The second source of comfort in the wilderness is what I call "The Help." For all you movie buffs out there, I'm not talking about Aibileen and Minny. I'm talking about angels. We don't like to talk about angels in our culture. We downplay the importance of their role in ministering to the saints of God. But they exist. Not only do they exist, they support us in the wilderness. The writer of Hebrews tells us as much when he rhetorically asks, "Are they not all ministering spirits sent out to serve for the sake of those who are to inherit salvation?" (Hebrews 1:14). So be grateful for "The Help" God sends your way. It will help sustain you in the wilderness.

> *I'm not sure if you were looking to perform miracles first. Maybe you were looking to do great things for the kingdom of God. That's all fine and dandy. But let me just tell you, you are not exempt from the call to the wilderness. You'll find strength there. You'll find faith there. And most of all, you'll find God there with you every step of the way.*

"Behold, I am with you always, to the end of the age." (Matthew 28:20)

Day 13

Exposed

It has been well documented that the greatest fear people have is the fear of public speaking. There's something paralyzing about standing up in front of a crowd. All those eyes on us at once. What if we fail? We don't like to be exposed. We don't like to be vulnerable. Today we throw around words like "transparent" and "real," but when it really gets down to it, we hate being exposed. We also hate exposing things when we approach God in prayer. Shame sets in. We feel unworthy and don't feel like he will honor our forthrightness. But the opposite is true.

In Luke's gospel, Jesus heals a man who has a withered hand (Luke 6:6–11). This man is in the synagogue with Jesus. The Pharisees are ready to accuse Jesus of doing something unlawful on the Sabbath, since he'd just shown them up on a previous Sabbath. There were thirty-nine categories of activities that were prohibited on the Sabbath. Healing was one of those categories—unless the situation was life-threatening. In fact, Jews were allowed to rescue animals out of life-threatening situations.

This man's withered hand? Not life-threatening at all, right? Try telling Jesus that. To Christ, he's worth more than an animal. His situation is life-threatening. He's created in the *imago dei*—the very image of God. He's wounded. His hand is shriveled. And it's his right hand, which is the most important hand in this culture. Jesus heals him. In one moment, he rids him of the very thing that's plagued his life for years.

Human-made rules required Jesus to wait to heal him, but God-led urgency necessitated that this ailment be dealt with. That's what Jesus does with our shame, guilt, and heartache. Culture teaches us to hide it. Exposing it leads to negative perception by others around us. Besides, our ailments aren't life-threatening, right? Those little sins aren't hurting anyone. But Jesus steps into our narrative and says, *It's crucial. It's life-threatening. It's paralyzing. It hinders your relationship with me. It has to be dealt with.*

We shouldn't gloss over this account without realizing the risk this man took. Jesus asked this man to stand up in front of everybody. Like a nervous public speaker, the man rose to his feet and stood next to Jesus. If that wasn't scary enough, Jesus asked him to show them all his withered hand. It was shriveled and atrophied. That's when the miracle happened!

The passage doesn't say that he was hiding his hand, but Jesus' request implies that he had it hidden. *Stretch out your hand. Take it out. Let me see it.* He trembled as he removed it from its hiding place. Maybe it was in his coat pocket. Maybe he had it hidden behind his back. Thinking about the way his hand probably looked, it was probably a badge of shame for him. He wanted to look as normal as possible in the synagogue.

Sometimes God requires us to expose the very thing we are ashamed of so that he may heal us. It's easier to hide it. It's easier to look normal. But Christ thinks it's crucial. He is Lord of the Sabbath (Luke 6:5). Stand up. Get next to Jesus. Stretch forth your hand. Expose yourself and he will heal you.

> *You should be careful about coming to God trying to look as normal as possible. Christians are good at this. Concealing pain, concealing heartache, and concealing hurt. None of this allows him to properly work to heal you. Though your God is all-seeing and all-knowing, it takes effort on your part to expose your pains and heartaches to him. If you're willing to stretch yourself, he will take everything that's broken and make it whole again.*

"Hope deferred makes the heart sick, but a desire fulfilled is a tree of life." (Proverbs 13:12)

Day 14

Touch

Research conducted years ago found that a warm touch tempers blood pressure and relieves stress. Nothing earth-shattering there, right? Ask any mother who holds her newborn against her skin immediately after an excruciatingly painful birth experience. Ask any father who comes home from a long day at work whose child immediately embraces him as he walks through the door. There's something about a touch that says, "You're special." When healing and affirming words accompany that touch, it can make all the difference in the world.

I am that father at the end of a long day. If my son merely greeted and hugged me, then walked away, though special, it's not as touching as him saying, "I really missed you today, Daddy," during our embrace. In that moment, all the stresses, unfinished work, and office problems melt away.

An unnamed man in the Gospels offers us a resounding "amen" (Matthew 8:1–4). With nothing to lose, he risked it all. His skin was literally in shambles. He was tired of being considered an outcast. His normal day consisted of shouting, "Unclean, unclean!" This was to warn others to stay away from him (Leviticus13:45–46). To others he was considered as good as dead (Numbers 12:12). His life was one of desperation. Untouchable, but longing to be held. Undesirable, but desiring relationship. Incurable, yet holding out hope that one day this nightmare would end. He had patiently waited for the mountaintop revival to end. He had seen others healed, biding his time. He hoped that his day would come. Then it happened. Jesus came down from the mountain (Matthew 8:1). That's when everything changed for this man.

Finally! The revival was over. It was now or never. Usually ignored by others because of his condition, this man had one last chance. His normal, limited, one-word vocabulary was replaced with a bold address: "Lord, if you will, you can make me clean" (Matthew 8:2). Others looked down upon his bold action. He was speaking out of turn. But Jesus didn't think so. Jesus reached out his hand and touched him. Touching him, according to Jewish law, would have made Jesus unclean. Touching anything unclean always made you unclean. It was never the other way around. But Jesus turns things upside down. His touch cleanses the unclean. This is the moment this man was waiting for—a touch from the master.

The story could have stopped there. Many had been healed by the touch of Jesus. For them, the touch was sufficient. But not this man. He was different. After Jesus touched him, he spoke to him. "I will; be clean." As soon as the words left Jesus' lips, the man was healed. It wasn't just the touch of Jesus that cured him, but also the words of Jesus.

Words. The same medium of expression that had previously betrayed him (remember, "unclean, unclean") had now healed him. If we could just get to a place where we move beyond the touch. In our hopelessness, we say things we don't mean. We say things we'd never say on a normal day. We start to see ourselves as unclean, unworthy, and unimportant. Like this leprous man, we see a visible reminder of this pattern every day. Whether it be a failed business venture, financial loss, or loss of a loved one, it's in our face every day. *Unclean*. We can create a pattern. Saying the same thing for so long that we actually believe it. The Jews believed that cures for lepers were just as difficult as resurrections from the dead. It's a good thing that the One who is the resurrection and the life showed up and changed this man's life (John 11:25). And he does the same things for us today.

> *When you move beyond the touch, your vocabulary will start to change. When you turn to Jesus' words, your hope is renewed. That's when you are assured that all things work together for your good. You become confident that he is with you, even until the*

end of time. You confide in the fact that he has left his peace with you, even in your apparent turmoil. Like this leprous man, no matter the circumstance, you can declare, "Cleaned!" God is looking for people who are bold enough to move beyond the touch and trust the promises of the One who keeps them unconditionally. Are you one of them?

"Rejoice in hope, be patient in tribulation, be constant in prayer." (Romans 12:12)

Day 15

Tears

A rare thing happened one day when I was living in sunny Southern California. It rained. Contrary to Tony, Toni, Tone's assessment that it never rains in Southern California, it rained all day Friday and all day Saturday. It rained like cats and dogs. Little did I know that this rain would serve as a precursor for a spiritual storm in my own life. My maternal grandfather passed away that Saturday morning. He'd been hospitalized a week prior. We knew his condition was getting worse, so we were prepared for the loss. But it still hurt. My mom was hurt. This was her father. I was hurting for her because I know that she cared for her father deeply. She was a daddy's girl.

I am not really the typical "black" movie genre fan. But one movie in the genre that I can really say I enjoyed is *Waiting to Exhale*. One of the most pivotal moments in the film for me was when Bernie (played by Angela Basset) was sitting at home with her daughter. In the scene, her daughter points to the glass ceiling as the rain stops and says, "Look, mama, God has stopped crying."

This reminded me of the tales and legends I heard from older people growing up. When I was a kid, older relatives would tell me that thunder was God bowling in heaven and rain was God crying. If it was pouring down, then God must have been really sad. As a young child, imagining rain as God's tears helped me understand that he really does understand our losses. As an adult, his tears still capture his compassionate heart.

"Jesus wept" (John 11:35). This verse is the shortest verse in the English version of the Bible. Every time we had to say a Bible verse in Sunday school, we used to jockey for position to be the first in line just so we could utter these two words. "Jesus wept" was the Beverly Hills of Scripture for Sunday school children—prime real estate. It was easy to remember and hard to get wrong.

I didn't know the power of this verse until I got older. Jesus didn't just weep to be weeping. He wept because he lost someone that he loved dearly—Lazarus. *Jesus cried? But isn't Jesus God? Why would he cry?* The author of Hebrews explains it clearly for us. "For we do not have a high priest who is unable to sympathize with our weaknesses, but one who in every respect has been tempted as we are..." (Hebrews 4:15).

Our losses sometimes make us presume that God is an otherworld being who cannot sympathize. We can forget that Jesus himself experienced a great, personal loss in his life. As he grieved the loss of Lazarus, the people asked the same questions we often ask surrounding our losses: "Could not he who opened the eyes of the blind man also have kept this man (person) from dying?" (John 11:37).

I know I've asked this question before. Why? I know you can do all things, God, so why not save my loved one? And then other Christians try to help and get spiritual on me. *Everything happens for a reason, right?* Where is that verse in the Bible? Where did we get that phrase? Not that I don't agree (and we can infer from Scripture that God is sovereignly in control), but people who are grieving don't really want to hear that in their moment of loss. Many of them already know this. More than anything, they want a listening ear, a helping hand, or an available shoulder.

So that's what I did for my mother when I went home for my grandfather's home-going. I didn't go through a sermonette. I did what I should have done. I was there for her to lend a hand, shoulder, or an ear.

Okay, let's be real though. Jesus raised Lazarus from the dead, so his pain was temporary, right? Yes, this is true. But I believe Jesus did this to demonstrate that our own pain is temporary. Days prior, Jesus had been told that Lazarus was sick, but he didn't come see him then. Why not? It's certainly easier to heal a disease than to raise someone from the dead. Maybe Jesus wanted to experience the loss we all experience at some point in our lives. Maybe he wanted to silence all the critics who wanted to say he didn't understand. Jesus showed up at a graveside, wept uncontrollably, and said, "I do understand." He can sympathize with us in our time of loss. That's something we can put our hope in.

> *Maybe that weekend rain was a subtle reminder from Jesus that he felt my family's pain. Today, I want to remind you that he can relate to every pain that you go through. As much as it may hurt, as much as it may feel horrible, bless God for knowing that God will give you the strength to look up, point up, and say, "Look, mama, God has stopped crying." And that's Good News.*

"For we do not have a high priest who is unable to sympathize with our weaknesses, but one who in every respect has been tempted as we are, yet without sin." (Hebrews 4:15)

Day 16

Obscurity

We live in a platform-driven society. Whether you're an aspiring author, musician, or pastor, there are many books dedicated to building one's platform. Build your tribe. Increase your follower count. Get more likes. Get more shares. This is a difficult place for many Christians. Christian platform seems like an oxymoron. Aren't we supposed to be increasing his follower count? Aren't we supposed to be sharing the gospel with others? Aren't we supposed to build his kingdom? Contentment is difficult in a society that keeps us in discontent, focused on ourselves. Obscurity is difficult to swallow when inundated with a message telling us to build our own platform.

Contentment. Obscurity. The message is counter-cultural. When media frequently portrays the fabulous life, you can't blame people for desiring that kind of lifestyle. Even Christians desire the fabulous life. When we don't experience it, we lose hope. And we ask the obvious questions: *Why am I not being blessed? What am I doing wrong?* What if the key to God's kingdom is found in the not-so-fabulous life? What if the key to God's kingdom is found in obscurity?

Take your mind back to the streets of ancient Capernaum, Galilee, and Cana. Barefoot, with one outfit, a carpenter from Nazarene traversed the Mediterranean in relative obscurity. Sure, he recruited twelve men to follow him. Sure, crowds followed him, but they were fickle and never stuck around. They were only in it for the miracles. It wasn't until Jesus began his public ministry that people began to talk about him in the upper echelon of Jewish culture. And even then it was to complain that he spent his time communing with vagabonds, sinners, and prostitutes. Anyone who would associate with these people had no aspiration to "make it" in Jerusalem. He was going about it all wrong. He wasn't building his platform the right way.

The religious leaders had the right idea. They had arrived. They were the platform gurus, sitting in the preferred places of society. They knew what it took to get ahead, and this Jesus of Nazareth was not going about it the right way. They recognized him, but it was for his quirky, counter-cultural ways. Even with this newfound recognition, he desired to remain in relative obscurity, stealing away from the crowds in solitude for days. Christ's platform was birthed out of his obscurity and obedience.

The people wanted to forcefully take Jesus and make him king (John 6:15). And what did he do? He withdrew to a place by himself to pray. Jesus was consumed by the will of God. His food was to do the will of the Father (John

4:34). He set out to bring God glory through his perfect obedience (John 12:26). That's kingdom-building, not platform-building.

Remember David's relative obscurity after he was anointed king? He was anointed king, but returned to be a shepherd. How did God know he was ready? David became a "man after God's heart," not his personal agenda (Acts 13:22).

> *The obscure life drives you from a platform mindset to a prayer-filled, God-seeking position. In the obscure life, God's will and God's heart consume you. That's the life that breathes hope into your mortal lungs. That's the life that is fulfilling. That's the life I encourage you to desire.*

"Meanwhile, be content with obscurity, like Christ." (Colossians 3:4b, MSG)

Day 17

Maestro

Tap! Tap! Tap! All of sudden, the once rowdy audience came to order. The chatter died down. It was time to start the show. The maestro had arrived. It was time for the concert to begin. There's something about the maestro's presence that brings order out of chaos. His presence says the musical masterpiece is now beginning. When the maestro shows up, the atmosphere becomes reverent. Like a king's coronation, he demands respect and attention.

Jesus is no different. He can make order out of chaos and qualm all our fears. He can eliminate doubt. But this only happens when we follow orchestral protocol. Let me explain what I mean. The word "maestro," of Italian origin, means master or teacher. Jesus is called master or teacher several times in Scripture (Matthew 8:19; Mark 14:14).He is the Great Maestro in our lives, tapping on the strings of our hearts.

The maestro's presence is commanding. He has the uncanny ability to maintain eye contact with his ensemble. Eye contact tells the ensemble that *I'm being attentive. I'm here with you. We'll make our way through this composition together.*

As Christians we know that Christ is attentive to every one of our needs. We know he has promised to supply all our needs (Philippians 4:19). But sometimes our own doubt causes us to lose eye contact with our Great Maestro. Ask Peter. In Matthew's gospel, he found himself walking on water (Matthew 14:28–31). Jesus had called him out on the water. And he started to walk on water—something that no human being had done in Scripture before. Everything was good. Until something happened. He looked down. Then he began to doubt the thing Jesus already told him that he could do. When he lost eye contact, he began to sink.

Peter's story is our story, isn't it? Jesus has bid us to come join him. He's given us permission to start a faith-driven journey. But we can get bogged down in the waves of life and forget about the necessity of eye contact. How am I going to pay this bill? Splish. Will I ever get married? Splash. When can I start a job in the field I really want to work in? Splash.

Any tightrope walker will tell you that the key to reaching your destination is your ability to keep your eye on the goal. Whatever you do, don't look down. Scripture records that we are called to "[p]ress toward [our] goal[s]..." (Philippians 3:14). Our goal? It isn't money. It isn't a bigger house. It isn't fame. It's Jesus Christ. Jesus is the end in mind that Paul talks about in Philippians. It's about us becoming more like him. It's about being transformed into his image and likeness.

Maintaining eye contact with Jesus is important when trying to eliminate doubt. Doubt kills our hope, like a well-placed poison trap in the corner of our souls. I don't care how well we pray, preach, or write. The key to our hope is keeping our eyes on Christ. Even the best musician in an orchestra can wind up a failure if he misses his cue from the maestro. Without that visual cue, the orchestra member doubts his role in the composition.

> *Where are your eyes? Where is your focus? Are you beginning to doubt your role in God's great composition? I want to encourage you to refocus on the One who wrote the piece and knows your role better than anyone else. Only then will you begin to eliminate doubt in your life and live the life that God has called you to live—a life characterized by the hopeful pursuit of Christ. You play an important role in God's work. Without you, the harmony is slightly off. Without you, the composition is incomplete. Stay focused, give the Maestro your undivided attention, and watch the masterpiece unfold before your eyes.*

"Then I shall not be put to shame, having my eyes fixed on your commandments." (Psalm 119:6)

Day 18

Between

Geography has always intrigued me. I love looking at maps and landmarks. During grade school, I'd spend hours looking at the classroom globe, feeling the contours that pointed out the various natural landmarks. Whether canyons, mountains, rivers, or lakes, you name it, I loved learning about it. One thing I learned during those formative years: Death Valley—the lowest elevation point in America—and Mount Whitney—the highest elevation point in America—are less than 80 miles apart. Imagine that. Going from a place so low to a place so high in just 80 miles. I'm confident that the start of the trip and the end of the trip would be exhilarating, but what about the in-between? It would be a grind. It would be unbearable. It would be painful.

The "in-betweens" in our lives can be just as painful, can't they? Think about it. You've had plans to do something that were derailed before, right? You've set out toward a goal before, only to realize that it wasn't as easy as you first imagined, right? How'd that make you feel? Let me give you a personal example.

When my son was an infant, my wife and I had the bright idea of driving from Georgia to Pennsylvania to attend our family reunion. We convinced ourselves that the 14-hour trip would be a great a time to bond. Wrong! Did I mention we had a one-year-old with us? What were we thinking?

Needless to say, bonding isn't exactly what happened. It was stressful. We were stopping every hour. I'm the kind of person who doesn't like stopping. I want to get where I'm going. You can't do that with a one-year-old. My son could care less about my preference to push through. *Forget that, Dad! I'm hungry!* The trip would have taken fourteen hours, non-stop, but it wound up taking us close to eighteen hours. I don't think I'll ever do that again. In fact, I have a "four hours or less" rule in place now. If we can't get there driving in four hours, we're flying.

Driving sounded like a good idea to us. We were excited when we left. And we had a great time when we arrived. It wasn't the launching point or the destination that was the problem. It was the in-between that was painful. As Christians we don't have a launching point or destination problems. Think back to that moment you accepted Christ. It was one of the most amazing moments in your life. You were starting on a journey that would change your life. The thought of experiencing eternity with our Creator gives us a hope and a destination.

But what about the in-between? There are some pit stops, aren't there? Disappointment Drive. Sorrow Street. Regret Road. We've all driven down them along the way. But are we really driving?

There's a popular bumper sticker that says, "Jesus is my Co-Pilot." Every time I read it I chuckle. It assumes that we're anywhere near the cockpit in our lives. It's self-centered, egotistical, and yields very little control to the God of the universe. The reality is that we're all passengers—in the back of coach. If I can take this metaphor a bit further, we didn't even start being booked on the trip. We were on standby until God called our names and brought us out of darkness, into his marvelous light. And here's the best news: he's taken the journey already!

At 1,200 feet below sea level, the Jordan Valley, just north of the Dead Sea, is the lowest point on the face of the earth. A little over a couple thousand years ago, God intentionally chose to enter his creation in a small town nestled in this same valley. That tears up our entire concept of God. If I was God and I chose to visit my people, give me Mount Whitney as my entry point. That's a little more dramatic, right? *I'm here! Worship me!*

But God wasn't looking for drama; He was looking to resolve our drama. To think that he intentionally chose the lowest point on earth to break through time and space to redeem us is humbling. Jesus was lifted up at the lowest point on earth, so we could be lifted up from the lowest points in our lives. Are you in Death Valley? Good. Remember Jesus' valley. Our low points pale in comparison to the low point in his life. He was stripped and beaten. He had his flesh torn to shreds. He did it because he loved us. But he also did it to let us know, "I understand what you're going through."

The Jordan Valley should remind you that you have a Savior whose experience was as low as they come. Jesus made his way up to the cross to give us a future and a hope. Today, ponder that promise and thank God for this reminder.

"Finally, brothers, whatever is true, whatever is honorable, whatever is just, whatever is pure, whatever is lovely, whatever is commendable, if there is any excellence, if there is anything worthy of praise, think about these things." (Philippians 4:8)

Day 19

Foxes

My first time in the Napa Valley was awe-inspiring. There were vineyards as far as the eye can see. Rows and rows of vines, ripe with grapes. They were ready to be picked. As I observed those vineyards, I thought of the vinedresser—the one who undertook the responsibility of caring for those vines. What was he like? How long does he spend caring for those precious vines? Who was this person who made sure they were reaching their full potential? I wanted to give the vinedresser props for his ability to take care of such a large number of vines. Then my mind went to Scripture.

Vineyard references are found throughout Scripture. Noah plants a vineyard very early in Genesis. Jesus taught several parables using vineyards as his geographic setting. Jesus tells his followers, "I am the true vine...abide in me, and I in you" (John 15). Scripture tells us that God is the vinedresser. The Song of Solomon uses another bit of vineyard imagery. Here, the author reveals the culprit associated with losing the expected harvest in the vineyard—the little foxes.

In biblical culture, foxes were sly creatures. They were the vineyard's worst nightmare. Foxes were opportunistic burrowers, so they lived underground. They took over abandoned burrows and made them their own. They were silent and lived solitary lives. In an agrarian society, they weren't very easy to detect. They dug around the grapevine, eating the plump, tender shoots.

Jesus figuratively calls Herod a fox in Luke's gospel (Luke 13:32). *Tell that fox what I said (author's paraphrase).* Strong language from Jesus, no? One thing about foxes: they know the exact time and place to pillage the vineyard—when the vinedresser was asleep.

The authentic Christian life teaches us that the enemy knows the exact time and location to attack. It's when we're most vulnerable, right? His suggestions might even be mixed with some truth. *You shall not surely die. You have the right to tell that person where they can go for treating you wrong.* Sly and subtle is his modus operandi. It's the little foxes. The little foxes can get us. They can rob us of our hope. But the Vinedresser offers us hope.

The closer you are to the Vinedresser, the harder it is for the enemy to attempt to steal your joy. Draw near to him and he will draw near to you (James 4:8). Unlike Mediterranean, agrarian vinedressers, God never sleeps. He alertly watches over his vineyard.

Can you rely on God? Yes. Want to know why? His eyes. His eyes run back and forth. Just looking. Looking to strengthen those whose hearts are fully committed to him (2 Chronicles 16:9). The task consumes him. This isn't a part-time job. He's not like, *I'll spend a few minutes looking to strengthen folks whose hearts are committed to me.* No. Every waking hour of the day the God who never slumbers and never sleeps has his eyes running back and forth throughout the whole earth to give strong support to those who are committed to him. That's what you need to remember.

How close can you say you are to God right now? Do an honest assessment. If the enemy can isolate you from God, then you become vulnerable and helpless. Of course, God is a present help in trouble, but if you are not submitted and close to him, then that Scripture means very little. Proximity to God naturally implies distance from the enemy. Draw close. The Vinedresser does his best work with those vines within arm's reach.

You also need to be aware that there are times when the Vinedresser needs to do some pruning. Branches are cut so that new, refreshed, fruit-producing branches may grow in their place. God may have cut some things out of your life recently that you've questioned. He saw something. Those branches were no longer productive. It was time for him to do a new thing. "Behold, I am doing a new thing" (Isaiah

43:19). So stop going back to that old source and looking for different results.

Lack of fruit indicates that pruning is on the horizon. Besides, the goal of the vinedresser is to maximize his return on investment. You can't expect the one who invested his life (on the cross) to be satisfied with your mediocrity and fruitlessness.

"For the Lord disciplines the one he loves, and chastises every son whom he receives."(Hebrews 12:6)

Day 20

Valley

I grew up with a ditch in my back yard. My brother and I used to go back there when it rained and try to jump across from one side of the ditch to the other. Sometimes we prevailed. Sometimes we failed miserably. We'd come home in soil-stained, water-soaked clothing, evidencing our unsuccessful endeavor. We loved it though. When water was in the ditch, it made things adventurous. That was during the rainy season though. During the dog days of summer, the ditch was dry. Not a drop of water. The same ditch that once revealed adventure became a steep, ravine-like drop that we did not dare try to clear. We were less daring during the dry season.

We're all less daring during dry seasons in our lives, aren't we? When things are dry in our lives, when the summer months come in our lives, we see the valley. It stifles our courage. We aren't as confident as we were in the past. Valleys have a tendency to do that. There's a certain risk attached to navigating valleys.

The Kidron Valley isn't any different. Situated just

outside of Jerusalem, the depth and angle of the valley—a 4,000-foot distance—caused the city and temple to cast a long shadow over it. It's so deep that many scholars believe Matthew is referring to the southeast corner of the temple, overlooking the Kidron, when he records that the devil took Jesus to the pinnacle of the temple to tempt him to throw himself down the steep cliff (Matthew 4:5–6).

The valley looks breathtaking from a mountaintop, but what about when your view is from the valley? John records, "When Jesus had spoken these words, he went out with his disciples across the brook Kidron..." (John 18:1). This was the final ascent of the King of Glory—an ascent that would cost his life. And the Kidron Valley seemed to be the perfect place for this ascent.

The Kidron Valley wasn't too far from the Holy City—and the Temple of God. This was the place of God's presence. What pilgrim wouldn't get excited looking up at the temple? Those making this trip could faintly see the brightly lit temple on the hill as they made their way through the valley. This was their hope as they traveled up to Jerusalem. *If we could just make it to the temple.* It looked to be just a stone's throw away.

But the Kidron Valley also wasn't very far from Golgotha, the place of the skull. The place that would come to be associated with the death of an innocent man—Jesus Christ.

Despite Jerusalem and Golgotha looming, the Kidron Valley became a present reality for Jesus. He found himself navigating this valley as He made his way to the cross. He moved through the valley and settled in a garden, the same garden he'd met with his disciples many times before. This time he awaited his betrayer—the betrayer who would give him over to be crucified.

So let's get this straight: a deep valley, lots of shadows, death all around. There's no commentary on Jesus' conversation as he walked through the Kidron. But he may have whispered these words: "Even though I walk through the valley of the shadow of death, I will fear no evil, for you are with me; your rod and your staff, they comfort me" (Psalm 23:4). It is said that David went through the Kidron as he fled Absalom. He penned Psalm 23 as a result. Shadows and death, but no fear.

Knowledge of God's presence has a direct impact on how you view valleys and death in your life. Valleys give you perspective. What's your Kidron Valley? A bad relationship? Death of a loved one? We all have valleys surrounding us at some point in our lives. And we might just have it all wrong. Just as many pilgrims would have said, *If I can just get to the temple*. Many of us today would say, *If I could just get to church*. But what sustains you in the valley? What sustains you until Sunday rolls around? Exactly what the Psalmist says: the presence of a God who led the Israelites daily in the wilderness.

Why don't you take time and whisper that prayer today. Look at your valley and begin to mutter those words: "Even though I walk through the valley of the shadow of death..." Watch your countenance change. You have a God who is guiding you through your valley. Let that renew your hope today.

"Even though I walk through the valley of the shadow of death, I will fear no evil, for you are with me; your rod and your staff, they comfort me." (Psalm 23:4)

DAY 21

Crucified

As of this writing, there are thirty-two states in the United States that allow the death penalty. In those thirty-two states, inmates sit on death row waiting. Waiting for the inevitable. Waiting to answer for their crimes. There are great organizations out there that work tirelessly to ensure none of these inmates were wrongly convicted. They work up until the eleventh hour hoping to secure exoneration for their clients. In some instances, they are successful; in others they are not. The work is both rewarding and disheartening. If you talk to some in the organizations who do this work, you'll discover that they've come to the harsh reality that they can't save them all. Though the evidence suggests otherwise, the system sometimes allows innocent people to be put to death.

Spiritually, there is not one human being alive today who has been wrongly convicted (Romans 3:23). Disobedience in the garden of Eden secured the death penalty for us all. Because of Adam and Eve's sin, all of humankind is guilty and sentenced to death, eternally disconnected from our Creator. From that moment, the death sentence manifested itself in many ways. Wars, murder, suffering, and pain all became a part of the human narrative. There's one death sentence implemented in history that stands out. It sought to remove any sense of hope from its victims. It was called crucifixion.

When people were crucified in the Roman Empire, they were often left on display for others to see. Nails were driven through the arms and legs of the victims, and they were subject to public display and ridicule for days at a time. Death was a slow process, caused by either shock or breathing fatigue. The victim was naked and vulnerable.

No doubt Paul had this in mind when he pinned these words in Galatians: "I have been crucified with Christ. It is no longer I who live, but Christ who lives in me" (Galatians 2:20). Paul rejoiced in the fact that he was crucified with Christ. But what did that mean? How does crucifixion inform our lives?

Though church tradition informs us that Paul was actually martyred for his faith in Christ, he talks in this text as if his crucifixion is a present reality. And for Paul it was. His proud, selfish, personal goals and aspirations no longer fueled his life. The work and will of Christ was his one desire. That's what crucifixion did for Paul. And that's what crucifixion should do for us.

Here's the conundrum of crucifixion. The Roman Empire used it to intimidate. They used it as a form of unbearable death. It was to remind people of their mortality. But God used it to remind us that there is a crucifixion that leads to life. The same death penalty imposed thousands of years before Jesus was lifted on the cross. We were exonerated in his sacrifice. Unlike the tirelessly working death penalty organizations, Jesus said while on the cross, "I can save them all." He restores our hope by absorbing the death penalty meant for us. Exchanging our sin for his righteousness. As we sat in the dark, dingy cells of our lives without hope, Jesus walked past the guards, entered our hearts, and said, "You're free."

That's the beauty of the gospel. All other religions say do; the cross says done. All other religions say earn it; the cross says already earned. All other religions are about human's strict obedience; the cross is about his perfect obedience.

Here's something else we know. Crucifixion made a person as vulnerable as possible. Can you think of any more vulnerable position than hanging naked, publicly displayed on a cross?

We don't like the word "vulnerable." We want his righteousness without the accompanying vulnerability. But if we're really crucified with Christ, we're called to be vulnerable. We're called to be open and honest in our relationships. We're called to be vulnerable when discussing our shortcomings with our God.

Sure vulnerability might experience ridicule. Sure you may subject yourself to public scorn, but vulnerability is necessary. (Regarding relationships, be discerning. Everybody you meet doesn't deserve your vulnerability. Some are good at taking advantage of it.)

When you get to a point where you want to come down off your cross, when you get to a point where Christ's finished work isn't enough, remember his sacrifice and his determination to go through with it so we'd be freed from the curse of sin and death.

"I have been crucified with Christ. It is no longer I who live, but Christ who lives in me. And the life I now live in the flesh I live by faith in the Son of God, who loved me and gave himself for me." (Galatians 2:20)

Day 22

Encounter

The cross means many things to many people. For Romans in Jesus' day, it was a deterrent. Criminals would be crucified on crosses to communicate one message: don't mess with Rome. Over time, the cross has found itself in a dichotomous existence. The cross became both a symbol of torture and a symbol of relief. It became both a symbol of intimidation and a symbol of hope. Ultimately, it became the symbol of Christianity.

We all know and remember Jesus' words to take up our own cross and follow him (Luke 9:23). The words intimate a radical call to discipleship that requires us to endure hardships. But what about the one who was required to take up Jesus' cross? What about the man mentioned in passing in the Gospels? His name was Simon, and he hailed from Cyrene. Scripture records the following: "And [the soldiers] compelled a passerby, Simon of Cyrene, who was coming in from the country, the father of Alexander and Rufus, to carry [Jesus'] cross" (Mark 15:21).

Here was a man who was minding his own business.

We're not too sure why he was coming into town on that fateful day. Maybe he was among the many pilgrims making the trip for the Passover. Maybe he was strolling through to pick up some turtle doves for his family. I'm quite sure he didn't have carrying the cross of a "criminal" on the agenda. Yet he was forced to carry Jesus' cross. He had no choice, but let's not trivialize his willingness to do so. It may be that he heard the Lord's instruction to go two miles if forced to walk one (Matthew 5:41). We're not sure. We know one thing. The day Simon encountered the cross his life was radically transformed.

Simon's name means"harkening, listening." I believe Simon lived up to his name on that day as Jesus trudged up to Calvary. In being forced to carry Jesus' cross, he was listening. He was listening to God's call to become a disciple of Christ. He was listening to Jesus' words that he was the door, the resurrection, and the life. Who knows what was going on in Simon's life before this moment? He may have been having problems at home. He may have been having financial difficulties. Whatever the case, this encounter changed everything.

The cross has that kind of impact. I recall countless stories of believers whose lives were changed the day they encountered the cross. In that moment, they realized the selfless nature of the work of the cross, contrasted by the selfishness that characterized their lives. They realized their utter depravity apart from the finished work of Christ. They realized their inability to do enough to earn God's grace. They realized the transformative power of what seems to be, at first glance, merely two planks of wood.

Early church tradition suggests that Simon's sons, Rufus and Alexander, became missionaries. Imagine them hearing their father's story growing up. *I went into town to grab a few turtle doves and came back having carried the cross of the Son of God.* I'm quite sure that story never grew old. One man's encounter with the cross led to generational encounters with the message of the cross. Never underestimate your ability to impact your family with the message of the cross.

> *The message of the cross can break generational curses. It can reconcile broken family relationships. More than that, the message of the cross spews hope. The cross may serve as the bridge you need to close the chasm that has existed in your family for decades. The cross means many things to many people, but there is one word that sums up its message: "transformation." Think about how the cross has transformed your life. I challenge you to share that story with someone you've never shared it with. In taking up your cross, don't ever forget about his.*

"For the word of the cross is folly to those who are perishing, but to us who are being saved it is the power of God." (1 Corinthians 1:18)

DAY 23

Mistakes

Mistakes can cost us. People are in prison today because of the mistakes they've made in the past. People are divorced today because of the mistakes they've made in the past. It's hard to move past mistakes sometimes. They can drain us of our hope. They can suck the life right out of us if we're unable to move beyond them.

Our friend Peter could tell you about his own mistake. It almost made him look like a traitor. And it almost sucked the life right out of him. Imagine the scene. A scruff, sleep-deprived Peter follows the entourage that is bringing Jesus to the High Priest's house. A week prior he had just fallen asleep in the middle of a prayer meeting in the garden of Gethsemane. This same Peter boldly stood up for Christ when the multitude came to seize Jesus—going as far as cutting off a man's ear with a sword (John 18:10).

The scene today is different. As the crowd pushed forward to their destination to bring Jesus to be accused, this same Peter was there. But when it mattered most, Peter followed at a distance (Luke 22:54).

When it seemed Jesus needed a witness the most, he followed at a distance. When the greatest of all opportunities to witness presented itself, he followed at a distance. When that same trusty sword could have come in handy, he followed at a distance. Jesus had warned Peter before that he would deny him three times. But Peter got spiritual on him."Lord, I am ready to go with you, both to prison and to death" (Luke 22:33–34). No way I'll deny you three times. Three times? Don't you know that I'm in this until the end? But when it got down to the nitty gritty, he only followed at a distance.

Can you imagine Peter in the moment Jesus looked at him? Imagine the intense staring match he had with Christ. How piercing that divine glare must have been, as to say, *I told you this would happen.* This must have been the lowest moment of Peter's entire life.

If he had a "do over," I'm quite sure he would have reconsidered speaking up. But he didn't. He had to live with his decision. For believers, Peter's denial probably goes down as one of the greatest mistakes of all time.

Many of us would like to think that we would be bold in that situation. No way we would deny Jesus three times.

What about when we do or say something contrary to the Word of God? Does that not effectively serve as a denial? *Jesus isn't Lord over my mouth right now. I need to say this. He isn't Lord over my finances right now. I just have to make this purchase right now.*

Fast forward a bit. After Jesus' resurrection, he sat down and had breakfast with his disciples (John 21:15–19). He asked if Peter loved him. Three times. Peter couldn't help but think, "He really thinks I don't love him."He said, "Lord, you KNOW that I love you."Despite my shortcomings, you KNOW I love you. Despite my inability to speak up when it mattered, you KNOW I love you. Despite missing the mark, you KNOW I love you. This was enough for Christ. Jesus responded, "Feed my sheep."

If you look at the rest of Peter's life, this was a defining moment for him. He spent the rest of his life determined to feed Jesus' sheep. No way he would miss the mark this time. Today, Peter is remembered as a founder of the Christian church and the apostle instrumental in the growth of the early church.

Mistakes hurt. They linger. They make us feel lower than low. *How could I have done that? What was I thinking? How could I have been so stupid? I can't believe I fell for that again. I really wish that had never happened.* Are any of those questions/statements familiar? I know they are for me. Like Peter, I have gotten to a point where I felt like my mistakes have disqualified me. In the past, I have felt like I was beyond the point of grace. No way Jesus still thinks I love him. No way I'm qualified to be a follower of Christ.

Here's an earth-shattering truth that brings us hope. God isn't interested in using us in our strength; He wants to use us in our weakness. That was Paul's boast. If I must boast, I will boast of the things that show my weakness (2 Corinthians 11:30).

What mistakes have you made? Have you felt that those mistakes have separated you from God? How do you feel about those mistakes? Do they lie dormant in the annals of memories past? Peter was frustrated because he denied Jesus when it mattered the most. He wound up proclaiming Jesus everywhere he went. Trust God in your weaknesses and he will show himself strong.

"If I must boast, I will boast of the things that show my weakness." (2 Corinthians 11:30)

Day 24

Friday

I remember when Good Friday was not too "good" for me at all. In my younger years, I spent one Friday afternoon playing softball on an intramural softball team. Why was I playing softball? I don't know. I didn't have a softball-playing bone in my body. But I was out there nonetheless. I was playing center field and someone hit a fly ball to me. I ran under it to catch it and I misplayed it (did I mention I am not a great softball player?). The ball went over my head.

As I ran to retrieve it, I stepped in a hole and severely twisted my ankle. I'd already broken my ankle several times playing basketball, a sport I'm more comfortable with. So the feeling was less than welcome. I got home and limped around my apartment all day Friday. I felt horrible. I hoped to wake up on Saturday rejuvenated. But when I woke up, there was much of the same feeling. My ankle was still killing me.

That same day, I learned that a colleague of mine had recently died of lung cancer. He was twenty-nine years old and graduated high school with me. There seemed to be so much pain surrounding me. So much death surrounding me.

Then a thought came to me. Could I be experiencing the same feelings that the disciples felt on Friday and Saturday of Holy Week? They had been walking with Jesus for three-and-a-half years. Then, all of a sudden, he was gone. They had left all to follow him. They had nowhere else to go. He'd been crucified and placed in a tomb. They saw no hope.

As Christians we have a tendency to emphasize Easter Sunday and him getting up. And rightfully so. The resurrection is the event our entire faith hinges on. In fact, Easter service is probably one of the most attended services of the year. It's full of hope, Easter suits, and Easter speeches. But we also have to realize the reality of our own Friday/Saturday experiences (e.g., experiences of pain, death, and burial). How do we transition from our own pain and burial to resurrection when things look so bleak?

In the Gospels, the government in power put Jesus in a tomb and set guards at the rock to make sure the disciples didn't steal his body. In the same way, there are rocks placed over the tombs of our hearts, closely guarded by the enemy. He challenges us to attempt to remove them ourselves.

And to be honest, many times we try to remove them ourselves. In my cozy apartment, I tried everything on Friday and Saturday to get over my sinking feeling. I turned on the television. I called a few friends. I sat around lazily browsing the Internet. I was trying to remove that rock. But it wasn't until I opened the Word on Saturday evening that I realized that my Friday and Saturday were necessary. No matter how painful Friday and Saturday were, I couldn't make it to Sunday without going through them first.

In a sense, it allowed me to experience what the disciples experienced. It wasn't until the disciples experienced Friday and Saturday that they understood what Christ meant when he said "it was necessary" for him to suffer and die (i.e., go through Friday and Saturday) to experience a glorious resurrection on the third day.

> *It is my hope you realize that you cannot fully appreciate Sunday until you learn to appreciate (and in some sense embrace) your own Friday and Saturday experiences. When I recalibrated my thinking, I started to look forward to my Sunday. It wasn't just because I was going to church. It was because Sunday served as a reminder for me. If he got up, then you can get up. If you are going through your own Friday or Saturday experience, don't worry because Sunday is right around the corner. And if you can look up, you can get up. That's a promise unique to the Christian faith. Jesus got up. And one day, you will too.*

"For as by a man came death, by a man has come also the resurrection of the dead." (1 Corinthians 15:21)

Day 25

Look

The mere mention of the word "holiness" invokes images of the heaven-rending. Most people envision a picturesque scene depicting God high and lifted on a throne. Angels surround him crying, "Holy, holy, holy is the Lord God Almighty!" If we ever get to a point where we wrap our minds around the holiness of God, then we'll realize just how unworthy we are to be in his presence (Isaiah 6:1–5).

There's also a flip side to this coin. Similar to the disciples in the first chapter of Acts (Acts 1:10), we gaze upward toward heaven and see an ascending Christ. And in the same way, we are gently reminded: "Why do you stand looking into heaven?" (Acts 1:11).

Sometimes we get wrapped up in God's holiness (and we should, since his holiness is unfathomable). It's amazing. That is, until we forget God's requirement for our own holiness. This might be what the disciples saw early in Acts. They were so wrapped up in Jesus' ascension and holiness that they nearly forgot there was a Great Commission to carry out. They almost forgot the commission to live a holy life in an unholy culture. They nearly missed their mission. The gospel may have never reached the ends of the earth had the disciples failed to realize something. While it's important to look up, it's just as important to look out.

Since the one who called us is holy, we are called to be holy in our conduct as well (1 Peter 1:16). Holiness is about being set apart, but not living apart from our society and culture. As Christians we love the fact that we are set apart. Sometimes we love it a little too much. We separate ourselves from those whose beliefs and values don't line up with our own. We find ourselves in little conclaves of safety, surrounded by others who believe the same things we believe. A little leaven leavens the whole lump, right? Why is it that we think about the negative impact others may have on us rather than the positive impact we may have him them?

Peter puts it well: "Live an exemplary life [a life of holiness] *among the natives* so that your actions will refute their prejudices. Then they'll be won over to God's side and be there to join in the celebration when he arrives" (1 Peter 2:11, MSG, emphasis author's). Did you see that? We are supposed to live our holy and exemplary lifestyles among the natives. Your holiness just isn't for you. Your holiness isn't just for Sunday mornings. Your holiness isn't just for church conferences or retreats. Your holiness is for others outside of the faith to see, ultimately winning them over to God's side. This is what brings the world hope. This is what Jesus meant when he asks us to let our lights shine before others. It ultimately brings God's glory (Matthew 5:16). When was the last time your conduct won someone else over to God's side? When was the last time your conduct caused others to glorify God?

Our lives are examples to those who have not embraced our values and faith. If we live upright, maybe then we'll begin to impact a culture that is becoming increasingly hostile toward people of faith. Outsiders observing holiness in God's people outside of the proverbial "four walls of the church" just might increase people's trust in the gospel and those who proclaim it. Holiness is, at its core, the demonstration of the kingdom of God on earth—among the natives.

> *God is holy. You are also called to be holy. But your holiness isn't to be bottled up and served up like a rare vintage wine; it shouldn't be reserved for the presence of God and God's people. Look up, but don't forget to look out. Like the disciples, have you spent your days looking up rather than looking out? Have you unjustifiably removed yourself from culture because*

of its potential impact on your holiness? Look out! This means looking out to a hurting, dying world. This means looking out and demonstrating a godly lifestyle to a society void of a godly conscience. Only then will we be able to fully comprehend God's command: "You shall be holy, for I am holy" (1 Peter 1:16). Doing just that will cause hope to arise in a lost and dying world.

"But as he who called you is holy, you also be holy in all your conduct, since it is written, 'You shall be holy, for I am holy.'" (1 Peter 1:15–16)

Day 26

Concealed

Growing up, I had a bootleg piggy bank (don't judge me). I took a two-liter Sprite bottle and slit a hole in the top so I could put all of my loose change in it. Day after day, week after week, I'd stick the leftover coins I had from my day in that little bootleg blessing. I also knew I had five siblings who knew how to unscrew a top off of a two-liter bottle of soda. So I went to great lengths to hide my treasure. I wanted to make sure no one knew where I hid it. So I'd conspicuously rummage around my childhood home looking for just the right place. And I found that place. When my bottle was full, I finally removed it from its hiding place and used my money to purchase something I'd really value.

What if God went to such great lengths to do the same for us? What if he cared enough for us to hide us because he knew our value? The apostle Paul says God does just that. In the first century, it was customary to conceal treasure in clay jars, which had little value or beauty. This was done so the jars didn't attract attention to themselves and their precious contents. With that in mind, Paul writes:"But we have this treasure in jars of clay, to show that the surpassing power belongs to God and not to us" (2 Corinthians 4:7).

Among Greek writers, there was an understanding that contentment in suffering displayed some kind of special power in the individual. Anyone who endures hardships and trials had a personal strength that was unsurpassed. But Paul tells the truth. The truth that we all need to hear. The only way we get through our trials is through God's surpassing power. Because of God's surpassing strength. In the very next verse, Paul goes through a laundry list of items he'd endured and the way that the surpassing power of God helped him endure them. Afflicted, but not crushed. Perplexed, but not driven to despair. Persecuted, but not forsaken. Struck down, but not destroyed (2 Corinthians 4:8–9). But he wraps those truths in this truth: only God allowed his earthen vessel to endure those hardships.

Don't ever try to endure a trial without God. You will fail. Our earthen vessels can only take so much. If we realize that it's God's surpassing power that gets us through trials, then we really discover what Paul means when he says we have this treasure in earthen vessels. We don't deserve God's surpassing power, but he cares enough for us to extend us that grace. That thought alone removes our despair. That's hope at work.

As Christians we're all vessels. We are vessels that

contain a precious message—the good news of the gospel. There are times when we are hidden though. Where God conceals us in a place that seems to have a little value or beauty. And hopelessness can creep in. You might be concealed in a state of singleness. Concealed in a rut of a failed relationship. Concealed in a job that seems to be going nowhere. Concealed in school while God prepares you for your future. Concealed in a financial bind. Be encouraged. God conceals the things he treasures in places that seem to have little value.

Re-examine where you are today. The Lord wants you to know that he placed you where you are because you are valuable to him. In Paul's culture, when people placed these valuable items in clay jars, they wanted to make sure nobody could steal them. Also, they wanted to put them in places where no thief would even think to look. Although the enemy has set out to "steal, kill, and destroy" you, rejoice in the fact that you have been hidden in Christ. And it is in Christ that you're able to endure all trials, heartaches, and pains. Be encouraged. Celebrate your hidden state, knowing that in due time, the Lord will reveal you.

"Become the kind of container God can use to present any and every kind of gift to his guests for their blessing." (2 Timothy 2:21, MSG)

Day 27

Adoption

As an attorney, I have spoken with a few clients who were looking to adopt. Some were stepparents who married someone with children. They wanted to adopt their spouse's child because they considered the child their own. The biological father or mother was, in most instances, an absent parent, refusing to support or visit the child, even though they shared a genetic DNA. There were other instances where couples look to adopt children. Some were unable to have their own children. Some had a heart to care for orphans. Whatever the case, I let them know one thing up front: adoption is a game changer.

Legally, when you adopt a child, you are essentially putting the world on notice that you will care for, nurture, and raise that child as your own. You're telling everyone that the child has the right to anything you possess. The child enjoys inheritance rights as if he or she were your flesh and blood.

What about when the Creator of the universe decides to adopt us? How much of a game changer is that? Paul incorporates this adoption language in his discussion about our status with God as father. Sometimes we can gloss over Paul's treatment of our status in God's household. He tells us that God predestined us for adoption as sons through Jesus Christ (Ephesians 1:5). In doing so, we move from children of wrath (Ephesians 2:3) to children of God (1 John 3:1). What a radical shift! What ridiculous grace! God changed the game through Jesus' redemptive work.

In the United States alone, there are over 400,000 children who are living without permanent families. Worldwide, there's an estimated 153 million orphans. I can't imagine the despair they must feel being parentless. Many of them hold out hope that one day a loving, nurturing family will adopt them. They longingly stare out of the windows of orphanages, hoping that the case worker would call their names.

Like orphans, we, too, stared out of the windows of our soul, hoping that one day we'd hear our names. And God entered our story. He called our names resoundingly through the annals of time. The despair we once felt in our parentless state at once is wiped away on the cross of Christ.

He understood what adopting us meant. It didn't mean filling out paperwork and going through court proceedings. It was much more trying. It meant he had to die. It meant he had to give up his life. It meant he had to sweat blood in Gethsemane. He understood that he was taking responsibility for us, which begs the question: Why are we always so concerned about our resources when we have a Father who is our source?

Through adoption, God has put the world on notice that we are entitled to everything he possesses. He will sustain us because he has adopted us. Scripture records that we are "fellow heirs with Christ," so we can enjoy the inheritance accompanying this wonderful news.

But there's a flip side. Your adoption should be game-changing for you. Do you know what Paul says in the same breath when he articulates we are fellow heirs with Christ? He says that also means that we "suffer with him in order that we may also be glorified with him" (Romans 8:17). Adoption isn't always pretty. It isn't always perfect. There are certain adjustments that children have to make now that they have new adoptive parent(s).

They have to shoulder the responsibility of being children. That means carrying the family name. Paul knew all about carrying the name (Acts 9:15). He carried the name of Christ with zeal and a passion that caused the gospel to reach the end of the known world. But carrying that name meant being beaten. It meant being ridiculed. It meant enduring multiple shipwrecks. All because he carried the name.

As adopted sons and daughters of God, life isn't always going to be pretty. But life can be lived confidently by putting trust in the sovereign Father who is loving enough to adopt us and call us his own. How are you representing the Father today?

"For you did not receive the spirit of slavery to fall back into fear, but you have received the Spirit of adoption as sons, by whom we cry, 'Abba! Father!'" (Romans 8:15)

Day 28

Chains

I got my first bike when I was about four years old. I loved it. I would whip around the neighborhood on my bike like I was driving a new sports car. If I really wanted to get fancy, I'd run over a soda can and make my bike a "motorcycle." Nobody could tell me a thing. I found something out one day that changed the way I approached bike riding. Sometimes, I'd ride my bike so fast that the chain would fall off. Without the chain, I couldn't move. Without the chain, I had no mobility. Without the chain, I couldn't make any progress. So I'd flip my bike upside down and put the chain back on. Once it was back on, off I went. Riding into the sunset.

Chains are also mentioned in Scripture, but they weren't for children's bikes. Let's talk to Paul about these chains. Paul writes his letter to the Philippians as a prisoner in the city of Rome. He'd already gone through his first missionary journey and was entering the twilight of his ministry. He had appealed to his Roman citizenship to the authorities at the end of the Book of Acts. And where did this appeal get him? Chained. In jail.

As a member of God's kingdom, our citizenship appeal often puts us in the same place. We are citizens of God's kingdom (Philippians 3:20). There are rulers and authorities that attempt to place us in chains. As Paul writes the letter to the church at Philippi, I'm sure the Christians at Philippi are thinking the same thing. *Paul is in jail. What are we going to do now? How will that affect the proclamation of the gospel?*

The Philippians were on the verge of forgetting what had happened at Philippi several years prior. Paul hadn't forgotten though. He remembered sitting in a jail in Philippi attached to his companion Silas. He remembered not being able to see the light of day. He remembered when things looked hopeless at Philippi. But he also remembered what God did. As he and Silas sat in that cell, they worshipped. As they worshipped, God moved (Acts 16:16–40).This is the same church that Paul writes to from a jail in Rome.

Paul's words are confident. *I know one thing, he says. My chains are in Christ. And they will turn out to further the gospel.* What confidence! What moxie! All the hurt. All the pain. All the disappointments. All that has happened to Paul would turn out for the furtherance of the gospel. How? It would become evident to others around him that his chains were in Christ.

Take Paul's words to heart today. As you move out of your own hurts, as you move out of your own pains, as you move out of your own disappointments, people around you will begin to recognize that it was Christ's presence in your life that sustained you. The same people who attempted to "lock you up" will begin to recognize the joy you had in the midst of the turmoil. A joy found in Christ. They'll begin to recognize the peace you had in the midst of the hurt. They'll begin to recognize the resolve you had in the midst of the pain. The palace guard will take notice. They don't have a choice. They have been too close in proximity to you not to recognize. They had been assigned to watch you. It's amazing that the same people who had been assigned to watch you will see the evidence of Christ's work in your life.

Many years ago, someone realized that linking metal together and attaching it to a pulley had a very profound impact. Creating these chains allowed humans to lift items many times their weight with little to no effort.

Our lives often carry a ton of weight. We're weighed down spiritually. Weighed down financially. Weighed down emotionally. But Paul reminds us that our chains were not in vain. God wants you to use those chains to lift things that you can't deal with in your own strength. He wants you to wrap them around his Spirit's pulley. His yoke is easy and his burden is light. Grab on to that truth today.

Embrace your chains. They are the exact instruments God may use to move you forward. Be encouraged by Paul's words. Your chains are in Christ. God will use your chains to develop your character. They will turn out for the furtherance of the gospel. They will be used for his glory.

"Count it all joy, my brothers, when you meet trials of various kinds, for you know that the testing of your faith produces steadfastness." (James 1:2–3)

Day 29

Anger

For better or for worse. Words most people include in their marital vows. But what we really mean when we say that is that we only want to see the better. We marry because of the better. Nobody goes into a marriage expecting worse. Nobody goes into a marriage expecting to be disappointed by a spouse's behavior. You certainly don't go into marriage thinking you'll get angry with your spouse—at least not on your wedding day. But those vows aren't just passing words to be said without serious reflection. The vows presuppose that worse will come. Sometimes worse will hit your relationships like a ton of bricks. And you better be ready. Otherwise unresolved anger will consume you.

I'm not naive. Anger happens. It's natural. In fact, God gets angry (Psalm 2:12). But the difference between God's anger and our anger is that his anger is not tainted by sin. We're sinful. Most times, selfish ambition drives our anger. I know that's the case for me. I get mad at my wife when we disagree on something. I get mad when my Georgia Bulldogs lose football games. Sometimes my anger is unjustified. I just want to be mad because I can. And nobody—I mean nobody—can change my mind. When it comes to my anger toward my wife, I spend hours on end not talking to her. I want to show her what she's missing out on. She needs to appreciate how great I am. She needs to know how privileged she is to have me in her life. She needs to know how wrong she is for not seeing things my way. All those thoughts are driven by my own selfishness.

I'm glad that God realized that there are times when we'll get upset. He recognized that we're human. This is probably why he had the psalmist write, "Be angry, and do not sin" (Psalm 4:4). Look at that. We have permission to be angry. We have permission to be, dare I say, human. But anger should never be followed by sin. What is sin? Holding onto that anger. Resenting a person for something they've done to you. Keeping a record of what someone else has done to you. True love keeps no record of faults (1 Corinthians 13:5).

I've kept imaginary score in my relationship with my wife. Any time she brings something up, my natural defense mechanism is, *I remember when you did this.* Then these words come to mind: be angry, and do not sin. I have to repent. Because a natural result of unresolved anger is sin. There's no getting around it. If you don't deal with your anger, sin is as much a certainty as the rising of the sun.

Sleeping with an angry mind is a nightmare for relationships. In that silence, so many thoughts come to mind. You think through reasons that justify your anger. You convince yourself to become even more upset. By the next day, it gets worse. The prophet Hosea writes, "For with hearts like an oven they approach their intrigue; all night their anger smolders; in the morning it blazes like a flaming fire" (Hosea 7:6). *In the morning it blazes like a flame of fire.*

On Sunday October 8, 1871, a fire began in the city of Chicago. It burned for two days, destroying over three miles of city property, making it one the largest natural disasters of the nineteenth century. What started out as a small fire destroyed everything in its path. The city was primed and ready for the fire. Most of the homes were made of highly flammable wood. The sidewalks were made of wood. Roofs on buildings were made of highly flammable tar or shingle. Because the environment was ripe for its spread, the fire destroyed most of the city.

That's what anger does. It takes your ripe environment—an environment that's highly flammable—and spreads. And spreads. And spreads. Until it destroys our relationships. Until we're left with nothing but dead wood and debris. Often, the fire starts in our mouth (James 3:5–6). Speaking from a place of anger causes us to say things we really don't mean. Think about those things you've said when you've been upset with someone else. Roman poet Horace is said to have penned these words: "Once a word has been allowed to escape, it cannot be recalled." We can't take those things back, can we? And the damage is sometimes irreparable. This is why we must carefully approach conversations when we are angry. It's true that anger lodges in the hearts of fools (Ecclesiastes 7:9).

As a Christian, will you still get upset? Yes. Do I still get mad when Georgia loses another big game? Of course. Do I still get bothered by some of the things my wife does? Yes. But I've made up in my mind—in the grand scheme of things—that I can't dwell on those things.

Christians like to sing about moving forward, but we refuse to do it in our relationships. I dare you. I challenge you. You have permission to get mad, but you don't have permission to stay there. Staying there gives the devil an opportunity to negatively impact your thoughts and relationships. It gives that small fire a chance to spread and destroy your relationship. Today, work on your anger. No matter how small the disagreement, don't allow anger to consume your heart. In doing so, you actively resist the devil and your hope will be restored.

"Be angry and do not sin; do not let the sun go down on your anger, and give no opportunity to the devil." (Ephesians 4:26–27)

Day 30

Shine

It started at 6:00 a.m. I heard the pitter-patter of the little guy's feet walking across our living room floor, as my built-in alarm clock enters my bedroom. Over the past several weeks, he'd discovered something. Walking in the room and standing near the bed wasn't enough to get Daddy up. He had to do something more drastic. Something epic. And he figured it out. Darkness means sleep. Light means wake up. So every morning he comes in and flips our light switch. *Wake up! It's morning time.* One day, I decided to interrupt his routine. The light switch in our room is connected to a lamp near my side of the bed. I removed the bulb from the lamp the night before. The next morning, as he routinely did, he walked in and flipped the switch. Nothing. He turned it off and on several times. Still nothing. *What's wrong? The only way I can let Daddy know it's morning is for this light to shine.* Even my three-year-old figured out this simple truth: light is a slumber-awakening, darkness-encompassing, morning-alerting sign.

Just as John does in Revelation when describing the New Jerusalem, we close this book with that truth. In Revelation

21, John is describing the majesty of the heavenly city. It's magnificent. It has precious jewels and gold streets, and it is surrounded by great gates (Revelation 21:10–21). All of this beauty pales in comparison to what John describes next. "And the city has no need of sun or moon to shine on it, for the glory of God gives it light, and its lamp is the Lamb" (Revelation 21:23). No sun. No moon. Just the glory of God and the Lamb of God. The same presence that lit the Israelites' camp with a pillar of fire and the same presence found between the cherubim in the holy of holies will one day light this heavenly city.

Our earth today depends on the sun and the moon for light. The same sun and the moon that God spoke into existence in Genesis. But the new earth will be different. Light has shined into darkness (John 1:5). Jesus, the true light, has become our slumber-awakening, darkness-encompassing, morning-alerting sign. He's awakened our hearts. He's flipped the switch on our cold, dark souls. That light has become a beacon of hope in this dying world. *Wake up! It's morning time.*

Heaven is completely Christ-centered. He is the lamp that lights the city. He is the Bright and Morning Star. The Alpha and Omega. In our pain, in our heartache, let us remember this. A Christ-centered perspective on suffering brings us hope. Most of all, it brings us light. Today, allow Christ to walk across your life and flip the switch. When you do, you'll find that glimmer of hope you were looking for all along.

> *John's point as he closes what we know to be the canon of Scripture is to contrast what we will one day enjoy with what we now experience. Today, we experience darkness, don't we? This entire book has been dedicated to encountering that darkness and illuminating the light of our hope, Christ Jesus, on it. And this holy city in Revelation brings us our final ray of hope. It's nothing like our present circumstances. No sun. No moon. No temple. No church. No sacrifice. No sin. No sickness. No disease. No death. No loss. No disappointment. Just Him. Lighting our souls. Eternal joy with our Creator. We read this and repeat the words of John in closing Revelation: "Come, Lord Jesus!"*

"The light shines in the darkness, and the darkness has not overcome it." (John 1:5)

Read more great stuff from John and watch encouraging video messages on his personal blog:

www.johnrichardsjr.com

Connect at:

Website: johnrichardsjr.com

Twitter: @brotherpreacher

Facebook: brotherpreacher

Google +: JohnCRichardsJrEsq

YouTube: brotherpreacherjohn

Vimeo: brotherpreacher

Instagram: johncrichards

www.ingramcontent.com/pod-product-compliance
Lightning Source LLC
Chambersburg PA
CBHW060511030426
42337CB00015B/1852

* 9 7 8 0 6 1 5 9 7 1 8 8 9 *